SECRETS OF A

DEAL'IONAIRE

CREATING WEALTH ONE SMALL DEAL AT A TIME

JOHN LEE

Secrets of a Deal'ionaire

THE BEST INVESTMENT ON EARTH IS EARTH...

~ *LOUIS GLICKMAN* ~ REAL ESTATE INVESTOR & PHILANTHROPIST

Acknowledgement and Dedication

There are so many people to thank for helping me get these words down on paper. First is my extraordinary girlfriend Laura Abeckerle (now my wonderful wife *Laura Lee*). This book would not have been possible without her. She painstakingly and patiently sifted through all of my chaos making sense out of it and making it "pretty." Laura is dearly loved and appreciated.

A special thanks to my mother and father, Marie and John Lee. Without them I would not be here. They have always given me encouragement to do things on my own and for myself. While growing up back in the 1960's, most of my friend's dads had "jobs." My father owned a music store and made his own way. Because of his influence I knew I would be an entrepreneur even before I ever heard of the word.

Next I would like to acknowledge my many mentors. I have been fortunate enough to learn from some of the best and most brilliant people on the planet. There are too many to mention and I don't want to miss anyone. There is just not enough room to name them all. I've expanded on a couple of them in chapter two, "*Deal'ionaires* Simple Plan for Success."

Another special group of people I would like to thank are my "encouragers", my good friends who kept encouraging me through my thick and thin times. Particularly I want to thank AJ Rassamni, Cynthia Schmidt and Terry Hall. These friends saw the big picture even when I was looking at the little picture.

A very special person that made all of this "reader friendly" is my editor Meg Stefanac. A tremendous amount of credit goes to Meg for making all of this understandable.

Also my artist Brenda Hite needs to be mentioned. She did a great job designing and working with me on the cover.

There are many other people that had a part in making this happen that I want to thank. Even though I may not have mentioned you by name, you have not been forgotten and are very much appreciated. Thank you!

This book is dedicated to ALL of the current and future *Deal'ionaires* in the world.

Foreward by Robert G. Allen

For years I have been writing, speaking and teaching about how anyone can build up wealth through real estate investments. And it's true. Anyone can.

I met John Lee a few years ago and have been impressed with his acumen when it comes to money and investments. Some people just have a knack for it, and John is one of them.

When John first approached me and told me that he had written a book about the methods he has used in his successful real-estate investment ventures, I was intrigued. Everyone brings their own personal style to the methods that I teach and I was interested to see how John would present his take on it.

I thoroughly enjoyed reading his work. John has picked up a lot of information while attending several real-estate seminars, reading books, networking and basically picking up knowledge from every source available to him. From the things he has learned from various investors and real-estate gurus, he has created a hybrid of the methods and ideas and developed it into his own personal style of approaching the real-estate investment market.

In this book, John shares and explains his methods in a clear, easy-to-understand narrative that literally anyone can follow. I particularly appreciate the ways that John has adjusted and adapted his methods to meet changes in the real-estate market and technological advances.

John is the Deal'ionaire. There is nobody that you know who has bought more properties than him. Thousands of little deals. I am excited about John. He has an incredible concept in Real Estate. There is only one Deal'ionare in the world and that is John Lee. You need to go to the workshop that John is teaching. It is remarkable.

There is absolutely money to be made in the world of real estate. John and I both know it and we want you to know it too.

The Best to Your Success and Your Investments.

Robert G. Allen, Author of The One Minute Millionaire

Table of Contents ~ Secrets of a Deal'ionaire

Creating Wealth One Small Deal at a Time

About the Author

John R. Lee has been working in the financial services industry for more than 25 years. This includes more than ten years' experience working as a mortgage broker with a focus on nonconforming borrowers and lenders.

For the past several years, John has been working as a full-time real estate investor. In addition to owning several rental units, he is constantly buying and selling properties for profit. He has become very knowledgeable about how to buy properties for back taxes without ever going to tax-sales. Through his ongoing education, John continues to add to his tremendous success.

John's innovative debt-elimination and education program has helped many individuals who previously thought they were credit-impaired. Now, John is dedicated to helping others succeed by teaching them how they can aggressively apply his time-tested, step-by-step real estate techniques.

If you have any comments or questions or would like information about upcoming books, CDs, DVDs or seminars, please send your inquiries to John at: thedealionaire@gmail.com

Chapter One
From $400 to $4,400 in 40 Days

THOSE WHO DON'T KNOW HOW TO PROPERLY ANALYZE, ENTER
AND EXIT REAL ESTATE TRANSACTIONS THINK TODAY'S MARKET IS
RISKY. THOSE WHO FULLY UNDERSTAND THE INTRICACIES OF
CREATIVE REAL ESTATE INVESTING CONTINUE TO PARTICIPATE AND
PROFIT...~WARREN BUFFETT~...

I have bought *and* sold more than a thousand
properties for back taxes and have never been to a tax
auction. As a full-time investor for over twelve years,
buying properties over the counter (with *no*
redemption period) has become my expertise.

Real estate is a game that can have different outcomes
depending on your choices. It is similar to a game of
Monopoly: when you get four little green houses you

can trade up to a red hotel. When others land on your space, you get to collect rent.

As with anything, one of the hardest parts of real estate investment is getting started. I personally engaged in interstate travel for more than two years before I bought my first property for back taxes, and the property ended up being right in my own back yard. What a waste of time. Through these pages, you will learn from both my mistakes and my successes.

At first, I over-thought everything. I was caught in a state of *Analysis Paralysis*, i.e. I got caught up in doing too much research. Thinking I had to know everything before I could get started, I ended up confusing myself—and a confused mind always says *no.*

The best thing that I could have done at that time was to just get in the game.

So, what's the point? As best-selling trainer/author T. Harv Eker says, *Ready – Fire – Aim!* Learn as much as you can and then take some action. This is the advice I should have followed. You can correct and continue as you go along. Sometimes, losing a little money can be invaluable as far as education goes.

The first property I bought for back taxes was actually in two separate parcels. They cost me around $400 combined. I put one up for sale on eBay on a seven-day auction and it sold for over $900. I knew I was on to something.

The second parcel, I sold in less than 40 days for over $3,500. That's $400 to $4,400 in 40 days! Not a bad profit. There were some costs involved, but making ten times your initial investment leaves a little room to work with.

These turned out to be the types of properties that I now specialize in. They are properties that *no one wants.* They will have been sitting for years as non-paying tax properties. I buy them and then find people who do, in fact, want them—and also make a nice little profit in the process.

These properties are mostly in rural areas. I particularly like properties in *lake communities*. They seem to be very plentiful and are easy to sell.

Today, a lot of people are selling courses on profiting through short sales, foreclosures, tax liens and tax certificates. The problem with these courses is that they focus on the *investment* rather than on the *properties*.

They say things like: "When you pay tax liens you will get the property *free and clear*, wiping out all other liens." The truth is, you may or may not take ownership to a property free and clear, depending on the county. There are ways to ensure a clear title to the property, which I will get into later.

Many courses also say things such as: "Government guaranteed interest up to 50%!" Sounds great, doesn't it? While you *can* earn interest on the money you invest in others' delinquent taxes, this money is collectable only if and when the property owners pay their back taxes. Also, individual counties set the amount of interest that is paid to the investor.

Well that's all fine if you want interest. I'm not interested in interest, and I do not want to play a waiting game.

I buy properties for back taxes because I want to own the property. I do not want the uncertainty that goes with potentially collecting interest from a delinquent tax-payer. In that case, you may be awarded the property if the owners do not redeem their property by paying their back taxes. I want the property now. This is why I prefer the immediacy of paying cash *over-the-counter* for properties.

Properties held by county governments are sold over-the-counter quite simply because these administrations need the money for their budgets. There are many things that county governments provide that we may take for granted. We all drive on roads and walk on sidewalks. We enjoy police and fire protections. Some of us love to go to parks. We generally have great schools that educate our little learners. The list goes on.

Not all counties sell over-the-counter, however. I have found that it is much easier to work exclusively with the ones that do.

According to 2007 Census of Governments, there are 3,033 organized county or county-equivalent governments in the United States. Within these counties, there are thousands of properties that are not sold at the tax-sale auctions each year.

County governments are always going to require tax money. Furthermore, they are reliable entities from which to buy properties. Because of the consistent nature of counties as tax-collectors and service-providers within the balanced-and-checked government of the United States, they are a proven safe investment.

How to Obtain a Property for Back Taxes

Each county in the United States has a different procedure for dealing with delinquent-tax properties. Many have periodic *tax sale auctions*. I have never been to one.

Thanks to the internet, it is rather easy to obtain contact information for a given county's tax collector. I will call them directly and ask if there are any properties available that did *not* sell at the last tax-sale. Depending on the day, they will either tell me that they do or do not have properties for sale.

And persistence pays off. You can call the same tax-collector's office on three different days and receive three completely different answers. This is not to say that the tax-collector doesn't want to help; the person answering the phone simply may not know the right answers.

Most counties reassign their back-tax properties from the collector to a *trustee.* In this case, the trustee is the one responsible for selling the properties. The tax collectors can direct you to the trustees. They are not hard to find.

Once I find a county that has some available properties to sell, I request a listing. Some counties post their lists on their websites; some may have to email them to you or send a hard copy through the mail. Sometimes there is a nominal fee involved. Every county is different and goes by its own set of rules. Always be very friendly to everyone that you speak with at the tax office and county courthouse.

Once I obtain the list, I look at each property's taxes due, fees and legal description. Property listings will vary in how much information is provided; sometimes, they don't even include an actual address.

It can also get confusing if the county uses a different set of lot and plat numbers than the community does. Sometimes the community information will be included on the list, and sometimes it will not. After dealing with a couple of properties, however, it becomes much less difficult to figure them out.

Some counties may charge the tax amount along with various kinds of processing fees. Other counties may charge more than the taxes owed plus their fees. Still others may only charge a portion of the actual taxes owed and add their fees. Every county has its own way of handling the sales of these properties.

After selecting the property (or properties) I wish to purchase, I will pay the amount requested. County officials will then prepare and record the deed in my name. Depending on the county, this can take 2 to 4 weeks—or sometimes even longer. Once I receive the paperwork, I immediately start marketing my property (if I haven't started already).

Some properties I sell for cash and some I finance. Either way is fine with me so long as I have someone else paying for them as soon as possible. Similar to *flipping* a house, I want to make an immediate profit or start collecting payments as soon as possible. These properties are fairly easy to buy. The key is to sell them off quickly.

Selling the properties is not as easy for some people as it is for others, but it makes all the difference. I sell my properties a couple of different ways. The whole point is to turn a few dollars into many dollars with as little effort and risk as possible.

Chapter Two
Deal'ionaire's Simple Plan for Success

FORMAL EDUCATION WILL MAKE YOU A LIVING; SELF EDUCATION WILL MAKE YOU A FORTUNE...~JIM ROHN~...

The absolute, most important and life-changing thing I have done (and am still constantly working on doing) is adjust my mindset. The right frame of mind will take you wherever you want to go, while the wrong frame of mind will do just the opposite. Your mindset dictates your actions.

What a person believes can dictate whether he or she succeeds or fails. Like Henry Ford said, "If you think you can, you're right. If you think you can't, you're right."

Napoleon Hill penned *Think and Grow Rich* during the one of the toughest economic times this country has ever seen, the Great Depression. "Whatever your mind can conceive and believe, it can achieve," he wrote.

If you haven't read this book, do; if you have read it, then read it again. Every time I read *Think and Grow Rich*, I get something else out of it.

Continue Your Education

Learning is an ongoing, lifelong process. There are so many highly informative books out there that I often wish I could read like Howard Stephen Burg, the holder of the world record for speed-reading. He can read more than 25,000 words per minute! Yes, per minute! AND, he can do it with better than 87% comprehension! I cannot boast the ability to read at anywhere near that speed, but reading and learning *are* a very important part of my life.

I also love going to live events. There is something about being with a large group of *like-minded* people that builds a lot of positive energy. I enjoy networking with the other participants. I am truly amazed by the number of people I have met, become partners with on different activities and remained *lifelong friends* with as a result of these events. I have BFFs (best friends forever) all over the world.

In addition to the acquaintances I meet at seminars, I have several *mentors,* and I learn something different from each of them. There is always an experience or two that gave them the knowledge and expertise that they have today.

Every master was once a disaster. No one starts out as an *expert.* We all start out with training wheels and sometimes fall off of our bicycles; each time we climb back on, it gets a little easier. Before long, we find that we can take those training wheels off and peddle down the road.

I strive to *continue my education* constantly. Everywhere you turn, there is a lesson to be learned and I spend my time seeking out these lessons. In addition to reading books and attending seminars, conferences, trainings and boot camps, I watch informational DVDs, and listen to educational CDs as much as I possibly can. Over the years, I have spent an enormous amount of money on furthering my education. Has it been worth it? Yes.

To put things in perspective, what does earning an MBA at Harvard cost? According to Matt Symonds, Chief Editor of MBA50.com, a website dedicated to the world's outstanding business schools, earning a Harvard MBA currently costs about $168,000. And for those at <u>Columbia</u> or <u>Wharton</u>, earning this degree costs about $10,000 more! (*<u>MBA50.com</u>, March 30, 2013)*

By comparison, many of the programs and training sessions I attend cost hundreds, thousands and sometimes even tens of thousands of dollars. The main thing I look at is: What can I get out of it? Sometimes one little tidbit of information can make or save me thousands of dollars.

My method of obtaining an education is also tax-deductible. Most of my training directly benefits my company, so my presence is required (wink, wink). My company also requires me to have an annual board meeting on the beach. But that is another story.

The main benefit, in my opinion, is what these conferences do for me mentally. I love being around positive, motivating people.

Stay Positive

There seems to be so much negativity in the world these days. Everywhere you look, there is some kind of major stress or drama going on. That is why I do not watch CNN, a term I use for "Constantly Negative News," regardless of the channel it is shown on.

These days, when I watch TV, I want to watch happy things that will make me smile. There is always room for smiles. Smile at someone and there is about a nine in ten chance that they will smile back at you. Positive energy attracts more positive energy. What I give out, I receive in return.

Everything is energy, and energy is everything. You will reap what you have sown; you will get back exactly what you have put out. The Karma Café says that everyone is welcome. There are no menus. You simply get what you deserve.

We all create and tell ourselves our own personal story. We are who and what we are today because that is the story we have told ourselves. But these are only our stories so far. We have the ability to change our stories. No one can or will change our stories for us. As my mentor and friend, Doug Nelson, often says, "We can have excuses or we can have results. We can't have both."

Another of my great mentors, Harv Eker, has taught me that we can, in fact, have our cake and eat it too. We do not have to live in an "either / or" world. We can choose instead to live in an "and" world. How stupid it is to say that you can't have your cake and eat it, too. What moron said that? Would you get your

13

cake and just look at it? NO! You want to eat it, don't you? I know I do! We actually can have it all, and we can do so without taking anything away from anyone else.

Do Not Let Others Keep You Down

One of the first things I had to do for myself was learn to quit listening to all of the reasons why the things I wanted to do were not going to work. Most of our good friends and family members who are inclined to give us advice have good intentions. They sincerely want the only the best for us. Unfortunately, they usually do not know what they are talking about.

It is highly probable that those who are looking out for us have never done what we are looking at doing. They most likely are not experts in the investment arena when it comes to dealing with stocks, commodities, real estate, or business. These people may want things to work well for us, but at the same time, they have a tendency to plant a million seeds of doubt.

Our loved ones will want us to stay safe and secure. They may want us to blend in with the crowd. They will want us to be like the other crabs in the box. Let me explain.

In the Pacific Northwest, fishermen catch crabs in their traps. When they take them out of the traps they put them into open boxes. They don't need to bother with covers because the crabs won't let each other get out of the box. These crabs will actually let the others crawl and climb on them, but as they approach the top of the box, the others will grab the potential escapee with their claws and pull them back down.

How many people do you know who want to keep you in the box with them? Not that it's fair to compare people with crabs—although some of them are delicious and some are crabby...just kidding!

When you have other people's negative thoughts running through your head, you might find yourselves thinking, "Oh my gosh! What if I lose money? What if I get stuck with a bad investment? What will others think of me?"

What if? What if? What if?

Control Your Mindset

We often "What if?" ourselves to death. That has been one of the more challenging things for me to overcome. The little voice in my head can be pretty noisy sometimes.

If, right now, you're thinking, "What little voice?" that is the one. We all tell ourselves reasons why things won't work. My mentor, Blair Singer, does a phenomenal job explaining it in his "Little Voice" Mastery™ Mentoring Program. He is also the author of Sales Dogs, one of the books in Robert Kiyosaki's Rich Dad's Advisor® Series.

Blair is, in my opinion, one of the top trainers on the planet. If you get the opportunity, I would highly recommend his training as it will enable you to achieve a very high level of self-development.

We all have a conscious (emotional) and a subconscious (logical) mind. Our conscious mind encompasses our reality. It is what we experience and what we are taught. It is our safety, security, and comfort zone. Our "box."

Our subconscious mind, on the other hand, is our logic. When we go to sleep at night, it takes over and we somehow figure things out.

Our emotions can lead us to achieve results. Harv Eker, founder of Peak Potentials Training, calls this the Power of Manifestation. Your thoughts lead to your feelings, which lead to your actions, which lead to your results (T-F-A-R).

Have you ever suddenly remembered something like a song title or a trivia question in the middle of the night? That is your subconscious mind processing the information you were previously focusing on with your conscious mind.

Our minds can be trained to focus on very positive things. We have the ability to tune out the negativity and move forward regardless of the "CNN" all around us. All it takes is conscious awareness.

Be Good to Others

Let's get one thing straight: **It does not take money to make money. It takes creativity to make money.** No Money Down? Yes. No money down simply means it is not your money being used. Money still exchanges hands in almost every instance.

I owe a lot of gratitude to Mr. Robert Allen for his timeless classic, Nothing Down. In this book, the #1 Best-Selling Author explains in detail how to buy real estate with little or no money down. This book changed my life! In addition to providing a lot of great information, Robert Allen showed me how and why to become Enlightened.

This book taught me that the real estate business is not actually a real estate business. Rather, it is a people business. People skills are the most important skills you can learn. Be good to everyone and you will always come out on top.

I love to do lots of little deals. That's the Deal'ionaire way. I use a cookie cutter approach to assessing every deal. Everyone has to come out a winner or I will not do the deal. Everyone needs to smile.

My analysis is very quick and simple. I ask myself the following questions: Is it legal? Is it ethical? Is it moral? What would my Mom think about this? It's great to make money but it is also important that nobody gets hurt in the process.

Before agreeing to any deal, I consciously think, "What if EVERYONE was watching?" Hmmm! Everyone! Think about it. Not just God, Allah, the universe, or whatever higher power you believe in, but also your mother, your friends, your family, your neighbors…. Everyone.

Keeping this thought in mind has made me a better person. There is no grey area. I go with my gut feeling no matter what the deal. Always doing the right thing is dependent on always doing the right thing.

I had an appraiser tell me one time that some of the best deals I could ever do were also the deals I would never do. He is a very smart man indeed.

A conscience mindset is achieved on purpose. It is something that we choose to have. I believe that my current mindset can only come from within. I am my own worst enemy and my own best supporter.

We all have our own life to live and we are all influenced by other people we encounter. I don't believe that I can learn everything I need to know from just one or two people. We are all just as smart as those around us. We just all know different things. We can share our expertise and learn from one another.

Eliminate Negativity from Your Vocabulary

We are also influenced by the thoughts we have and the words we use. They have led us to where we are right now and where we are headed in the future. Our reality is a direct result of our thoughts and our words. Are you happy where you are? If not, one of the first things to look at is the words you are using.

Words are very powerful. They can work for you or they can work very much against you. I have found that the best thing for me is to use positive words. They are powerful for me.

The #1, bar-none, phrase to get out of your head is "I know that." Once you think you know everything, you quit learning. Your brain shuts down. You don't listen. You don't learn. You showed them, didn't you? I never want to be a know-it-all.

My experience is that I do not know everything. In fact, there is a whole lot that I don't know. Keeping this in mind, I make a conscious effort learn something very valuable from everyone I meet. This is why I believe that it's always good to network.

There are a few words that I have had to ban from my vocabulary and omit from my world. These words are very negative and can be game changers in life. Pure Poison!

Negative Words to Avoid

In my opinion, the negative words you need to remove from your vocabulary are: try, can't, and but. Let me explain:

~~TRY~~

Try. What a terrible word. "Trying" implies failure. When I hear someone say that they tried something, I know that they did not accomplish whatever it is they are talking about.

In the Star Wars movies, the character Yoda has some very good quotes. One of my favorite is in The Empire Strikes Back when Yoda is talking to Luke Skywalker and tells him:

> "No! Try not. Do, or do not. There is no try."

~~CAN'T~~

There is really no such thing as can't. "Can't" simply means you do not know how or you don't want to do something.

Whenever I catch myself thinking that I can't do something, I stop and ask myself, "Is it that I don't know *how* to do this? Or do I just really not *want* to? If it's because I don't know how to do it, what do I need to learn before I can proceed?"

~~BUT~~

Most of us walk around with a really big but. The word "but" just gives you an excuse for the first thing you said. Any time you use this word, you negate the first part of your statement.

Consider substituting the word *and* in place of the word *but.* This is an *AND WORLD*. Own what you say and take responsibility for your words.

Wimpy Words to Avoid

There are also what I believe to be *wimpy* words. These words have the power to contribute negatively to our mindsets. I recommend eliminating the following wimpy words: hope, if and problem.

~~HOPE~~

When you simply hope for something, it is still a pipe dream. It is way more powerful to *know* or *expect* that something is going to happen than to hope that it will.

~~IF~~

Don't ever think in terms of if something is going to happen. By replacing the word *if* with the word *when,* you will gain more control over your life plans. Don't say "If I make this sale..." Instead say, "When I make this sale..." Rejecting this simple little word has been a game-changer for many.

~~PROBLEM~~

Too many of us focus on the problems, whether actual or potential. By doing this we usually accomplish little more than attracting more problems. There are a couple of good replacement words.

Some people refer to *problems* as "*issues.*" Although it is a bit better sounding, it is still a little too negative for me. I prefer to substitute with the positive and powerful word, "*challenge.*" I like this word because I like challenges. One of the best motivators for me to accomplish something is if someone tells me it is too much of a challenge.

New York Times' bestselling author, Joel Osteen, calls problems "*tests.*" This is closer to the definition that I give to *problems*. We have to pass many *tests* in our lives to get to the next level.

There is always an important *lesson* to be learned from every so-called problem. No matter how small the lesson seems to be, there is always some value that comes with it. By learning from the smaller challenges the bigger ones become a little easier to overcome. As the old saying goes, "The higher the levels, the bigger the devils." Learn the lesson. Teach the class.

Conquer Your Fears and Aim for Success

Kieron Sweeney, international business coach, host of *KieronTV*, and one of my great mentors, has played a significant role in shaping me into the man I am today. He says, "When we are stuck at some point in our life, it is because we have not yet learned the lesson." We need to learn the lessons in front of us in order to move on in our lives.

One of the toughest things I have had to overcome for myself was all of the negative thinking going on in my head. I thought that I was a *perfectionist*. I thought that I had to have everything right and that everything could be improved by my way of thinking.

What I discovered is that this way of thinking actually turned me into an *"imperfectionist."* I wasn't truly happy with anything because I didn't find anything to be perfect. Wow, those were there some truly *negative* thoughts running through my head! Pure poison!

What I came to realize is that everything actually *is* perfect. Things are the way they are intended to be. It may not always be the way I *think* it should be, and that is okay because it is not up to me.

We all have our place in this world. My role is to do what I can for those that I care about. I care about everyone and want the best for all. When I spent my time finding faults with everything, it did no one any good.

I am constantly working on *reframing* my thoughts. I catch myself when the *little voice* starts to conjure a negative story. My mind is really good at *"what-iffing."* It is very easy for me to *"what if"* a situation to death if I do not consciously put a halt to that way of thinking before it can gain a foothold.

Maintaining a positive mindset is the one thing that I constantly work on. Do I have fears and doubts? You betcha! We all do. We are all built to experience the same emotions. We all have our fears.

The important thing is how we handle fear, doubt, rejection and all of the other negativity in our lives. Successful people have just as much fear as everyone else does. The difference is that successful people are the ones who do not let their fears stop them from working toward their goals.

I put a very strong emphasis on making sure that my dreams remain bigger than my fears. I work hard to avoid as much stress and drama as possible. One of the ways I do this is by avoiding a lot of what is aired on television.

TV is a major source of garbage. I cannot believe some of the things that people watch on TV these days. Stop watching news programs. The news is full of killings, robbery and disasters of all kinds. If it isn't a horrible tragedy, they don't air the story. Don't worry; if something is important enough that you need to know about it, you will hear about it.

Even the dramas and sitcoms that are on TV are unbelievable. What many think are good stories or are funny shows, I find to be an insult to human intelligence. And there are so many *sheeple* (people following the herd) watching this garbage.

I recently heard a seminar speaker comparing the size of a person's TV with the size of their wallet. The direct proportion is that the bigger the screen, the smaller the wallet. His point was that many people value mindless activities more than they value time spent bettering their lives.

As life-coach Tony Robbins says, "The only thing we have to change to get what we want is the story we are telling ourselves of why we can't have it."

Whenever things in my life are not going how I would like, I simply *change* my story. We all tell ourselves our own story. Why not make yours a *good* story with a *happy* ending?

Chapter Three

Secrets to Making Big Profits From Little Deals

ENJOY THE LITTLE THINGS, FOR ONE DAY YOU MAY LOOK BACK AND REALIZE THEY WERE THE BIG THINGS...~ROBERT BRAULT~...

The following is an example of how I managed to earn a large profit through a relatively simple deal. On the 9th of November, I bought a camping lot from a local county tax office for $258.26. Immediately upon the completion of the sale, I advertised it on *Craig's List*. This is the actual ad that I ran:

$2576 / 9100ft^2 - ☮ $28/month ~ Very Nice Private Camping L☺t (☮ Fall C☺l☺rs)

Very Nice Private Camping Lot.

Close to St Louis!

Lake Timbercreek ~ Blue Eye Missouri ... 14+ Lakes ~

Wooded ~ Private ~ Great Price And/Or Terms!

ONLY $1474 cash!

OR

NO Credit Check! ... 0% Interest ... $28 per month ... Total

$2576 !

☀ Have Fun in the Sun ☀

🐢 Enjoy the Fall 🐢

☃ Lots of Fishing / Swimming / Hiking / Relax ☃

✈ Picturesque Weekend Get-A-Way ✈

☆ Gated Community ... Small Annual POA fees ☆

☏ Call for more details ☏ 314 555 1717 ☏ or email

ams826 @ yahoo.com

☻ You'll be Glad you did ☺

The only other things I included in my ad were a few
pictures of the property and my contact information.

I immediately received about eight or ten inquiries by
email. Most were just shoppers. Then I got a couple of
phone calls, and a finally, a couple of questions in a
text-message. I get these more and more these days.

The good thing is that text-messages can be answered at your convenience and can also be a little more personal than email. The bad thing is I am a "hunt & peck"-texter. What I can say in five minutes in a regular phone conversation might take me half an hour to say by text.

The person who sent me the text eventually became the one who bought this property. This sale was unique in that I never actually spoke with the buyer until the day we met in person to finalize the sale. She had even given me the necessary information for her deed via text-message.

I usually give the buyer a choice on how they would like to handle their down payment if they plan to make payments. They almost always want to put more down than I would have asked for. If they insist that I give them an amount, I will typically ask for the amount that I had paid for the property. In this case, that would have been about $300.

I gave the buyer two options: she could make a small down-payment now and pay the property off over time, or she could receive a substantial discount by making an upfront cash payment in-full. Christmas was around the corner and all the taxes were due by the end of the month.

She sent me a text saying she wanted to go with the cash option and it would take her a week to have the money available. I said okay. As a result of her choosing this option, I gave her more than 40-percent off of my original asking price.

About six days later I received a text saying that she had the money and would like to meet. We agreed on a time and place and met the following morning, December 22nd, in a *Jack in the Box* parking lot. There, she bought the property for $1,474. I gave her a receipt and some maps, and she verified her deed information.

I prepared the deed and had it notarized at my bank at no cost. Next, I mailed it to the county recorder of deeds with a check for the recording fee. Once I'd paid the recording fee, the country mailed the updated deed back to me.

I made two copies of this deed. One was for my records. I have found it is always a good idea to keep copies. I have had instances where I've received erroneous tax bills many years after selling a property.

The other copy was for the Homeowners Association where the property is located. I always like to make things as easy as possible for those at the HOAs. They can make things easy for me, too.

I mailed the original recorded deed to the buyer for her records. And with that, I completed the transaction.

Here is a breakdown of my costs and profit:

Cost for the property	$258.26
Cost to Advertise on Craigslist	$0.00
Gasoline used to meet buyer	$5.00
Two tacos	$1.07
Ink, paper and postage	$1.00
Recording fee	$27.00
Total Money Spent	**$292.33**

Sales Price	$1474.00
Minus Costs	- $292.33
Net Profit	**$1161.67**

I also invested approximately 3 to 4 hours of my time into this deal—including the time it took me to consume the tacos.

Here is a copy of the actual deed I received from the county:

●●-60-●●-01-013●●●●00

TRUSTEE'S DEED

Under Collector's Third Tax Sale

THIS INDENTURE, made and entered into this 9th day of November 2012, by and between ████████████, Trustee, GRANTOR herein, for the use and benefit of the funds hereinafter mentioned, and Heartland Hideaways LLC a Missouri Corporation GRANTEE herein, of the County of St. Louis, State of Missouri. Mailing address of Grantee is ██████████████████████████████████

LEGAL DESCRIPTION OF THE PROPERTY CONVEYED HEREIN IS SET FORTH ON PAGE 2. WITNESSETH THAT:

WHEREAS, the County Court of ████████County, ███████ by an order of record dated the 1st day of February, 2007, a certified copy of which is on file in the Office of the County Collector of said county, did designate and appoint Grantor as a Trustee for the benefit of all funds entitled to participate in the funds entitled to the taxes against the lands herein described; and,

WHEREAS, the said Grantor has accepted said appointment and is now the duly appointed, qualified and acting Trustee for the uses and purposes aforesaid: and,

WHEREAS, the said Grantor, by virtue of the aforesaid appointment, is now and was at all the times hereinafter stated authorized to bid at all sales of delinquent lands offered for taxes, interest, penalty and costs, by the collector of said county, which had been offered for sale for taxes for two successive years next prior thereto; and,

WHEREAS, the said Grantor is and was at all the times herein mentioned, authorized to purchase at such sales all lands or lots offered thereat, necessary to protect all taxes due and owing, and to prevent their loss to the taxing authorities involved from inadequate bids; and,

3/30

WHEREAS, ▓▓▓▓▓▓▓▓▓▓▓ Collector of ▓▓▓▓▓▓▓▓▓unty, ▓▓▓▓▓, did on the fourth Monday in August 2011 offer for sale for taxes for the third time, the lands hereinafter described, and at said sale no person having bid therefor a sum equal to the delinquent taxes thereon, interest, penalty and the costs provided by law, ▓▓▓▓▓▓▓▓▓▓, the undersigned Trustee for the uses and purposes herein set forth, and by virtue of the authority vested in her, did bid and purchase the lands hereinafter described at a price not in excess of a sum equal to the delinquent taxes thereon, interest, penalty and costs provided by law, and the same were stricken off and sold to the said Trustee for the use and benefit of the following funds entitled to the payment of the taxes for which the real estate hereinafter described was sold as follows:

FUNDS	AMOUNT	INTEREST	FUNDS	AMOUNT	INTEREST
Road	2.21	1.14	County Tax	0.52	0.27
Cities			Health Tax	0.81	0.42
Schools	38.91	20.09	State Tax	0.25	0.13
Jr. College	4.18	2.16	Handicap Serv	0.81	0.42
			Sr. Citizen	0.45	0.23
Pub Fee	90.00				
Cert Mail	18.00				
Addl Fee7	30.00				
Clerk	2.25				
Collector	0.50				
Penalty	5.29		TOTAL	$194.18	$24.86

All of which proceedings are shown by deed from the Collector of said County to ▓▓▓▓▓▓▓ ▓▓▓▓, Trustee, dated the 16th day of December 2011 , and recorded in the Office of the Recorder of Deeds of ▓▓▓▓▓▓▓ County, ▓▓▓▓▓ in Document number 20▓▓-10▓▓.

WHEREAS, the said Grantor has been offered the sum of One Hundred Eighty-eight dollars and twenty-six cents ($188.26) by the said Heartland Hideaways, LLC a Missouri Corporation, Grantee, for the lands hereinafter described; and,

WHEREAS, the County Court, by order of record dated the 9th day of November 2012, has ordered the undersigned to sell the hereinafter described lands to the said Grantee at that price and sum, and to execute and deliver a deed therefor.

NOW, THIS INDENTURE, WITNESSETH, That the said Grantor, under and acting by virtue and in pursuance of the powers in her vested as hereinbefore stated, in consideration of the sum of One Hundred Eighty-eight dollars and twenty-six cents ($188.26), to her in hand paid by the said Heartland Hideaways, LLC a Missouri Corporation, Grantee, the receipt of which is hereby acknowledged, does by these presents, grant, bargain, sell and convey unto the said Grantee, the piece or parcel of land situated in the County of ▓▓▓▓▓▓▓, State of ▓▓▓▓▓ and described as follows:

▓▓-60-▓▓-01-013-▓▓▓.00
▓▓▓▓▓▓▓▓▓▓▓▓▓▓▓
LOT ▓▓ PLAT ▓▓

TO HAVE AND TO HOLD the above described premises together with all and singular the hereditaments and appurtenances thereto belonging or in anywise appertaining unto the said Grantee, their heirs and assigns forever.

IN TESTIMONY WHEREOF, the said Grantor has hereunto set her hand this 9TH day of November 2012.

_____ Trustee/Grantor

STATE OF ▓▓▓▓▓▓)
) SS
COUNTY OF ▓▓▓▓▓▓)

Before me, the undersigned, in and for said County, this day, personally came the above-mentioned ▓▓▓▓▓▓▓▓▓, Trustee, described in the foregoing instrument, and acknowledged that she executed the same for the uses and purposes therein mentioned.

IN WITNESS WHEREOF, I have hereunto set my hand and seal this 9th day of November 2012.

Notary Public
State of ▓▓▓▓▓▓

My Commission Expires:
Commissioned in ▓▓▓▓▓▓▓

▓▓▓▓▓▓▓▓
NOTARY PUBLIC - NOTARY SEAL
STATE OF ▓▓▓▓▓
COUNTY O▓ ▓▓▓▓▓
COMMISSION #▓▓▓▓▓▓
My Commission Expires: 10/16/2016

Here is a copy of the actual deed I used to transfer the property to the new buyer:

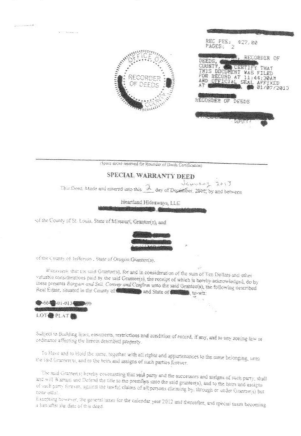

In Witness Whereof, the said Grantor(s) have executed these presents the day and year first above written.

John R. Lee, manager for Heartland Hideaways, LLC

STATE OF MISSOURI

County of St. Louis } ss.

On this __2__ day of ~~December~~, 201~~6~~, before me personally appeared

To me known personally appeared John R. Lee, manager for Heartland Hideaways, LLC, known to be the person who executed the within Special Warranty Deed on behalf of said limited liability company and acknowledged to me that he executed the same for the purposes therein stated.

IN TESTIMONY WHEREOF, I have hereunto set my hand and affixed my official seal in the County and State aforesaid, the day and year first above written.

Notary Public

My term expires: __4-25-2015__

In this section, I will give some examples of times I made an easy profit on a small investment.

As-Is House Sold Through a Realtor

In June of one year, I bought a house for back taxes from the county trustee. I sold that house the following May at a profit of $8,000.

When I bought it, the house was completely falling in. It was a total fixer-upper.

The following is a breakdown of my costs for the purchase:

County Taxes	$512.77
City Taxes	$759.16
Letter report from the title company	$125.00
Attorney fees for quiet-title lawsuit	$450.00
One year of taxes while holding	$187.41
Total Costs	**$2034.34**

I had originally planned to fix this house up and use it as a rental property. However, after receiving the quiet-title lawsuit judgment (see section on *Due Diligence*), I decided instead to sell it as-is.

I listed the house with a realtor and it sold within a couple of weeks. It was purchased for $11,000 and the check I received from the title company was for $10,034.48.

Other than my holding time, this was a very easy transaction. Not that the holding was difficult—it just took a while to get a court date for the quiet title. That does happen sometimes.

Once I had a sales contract, it was only a matter of showing up at the title company, signing some papers, getting my check and going to the bank.

Here is how the money flowed:

Check amount	$10,034.48
Total Cost	$2,034.34
Net Profit	**$8,000.14**

For this deal, I probably invested a total of about 8 hours of my time and used up about $50 worth of gas.

Here is a copy of my actual deed from the trustee

TRUSTEE'S DEED

Under Collector's Third Tax Sale

THIS INDENTURE, made and entered into this 13th day of June ▮▮▮, by and between ▮▮▮▮▮▮▮▮▮, GRANTOR herein, for the use and benefit of the funds hereinafter mentioned, and HEARTLAND HIDEAWAYS, LLC a Missouri Corporation, GRANTEE herein, of the County of St. Louis, State of Missouri. Mailing address of grantee is ▮▮▮▮▮▮▮▮▮▮▮, ▮▮▮▮ ▮▮ ▮▮.

LEGAL DESCRIPTION OF THE PROPERTY CONVEYED HEREIN IS SET FORTH ON PAGE 2.

WITNESSETH THAT:

WHEREAS, the County Court of ▮▮▮▮▮▮ County, ▮▮▮▮▮ by an order of record dated the 3rd day of June, 1975, a certified copy of which is on file in the Office of the County Collector of said county, did designate and appoint Grantor as a Trustee for the benefit of all funds entitled to participate in the funds entitled to the taxes against the lands herein described; and,

WHEREAS, the said Grantor has accepted said appointment and is now the duly appointed, qualified and acting Trustee for the uses and purposes aforesaid; and,

WHEREAS, the said Grantor, by virtue aforesaid appointment, is now and was at all the times hereinafter stated authorized to bid at all sales of delinquent lands offered for taxes, interest, penalty and costs, by the collector of said county, which had been offered for sale for taxes for two successive years next prior thereto; and,

WHEREAS, the said Grantor is and was at all the times herein mentioned, authorized to purchase at such sales all lands or lots offered thereat, necessary to protect all taxes due and owing, and to prevent their loss to the taxing authorities involved from inadequate bids; and,

WHEREAS, ████████████, Collector of ████████ County, ████████, did on the 1st day of December 2004 offer for sale for taxes for the third time, the lands hereinafter described, and at said sale no person having bid therefor a sum equal to the delinquent taxes thereon, interest, penalty and the costs provided by law, ███████████, the undersigned Trustee for the uses and purposes herein set forth, and by virtue of the authority vested in him, did bid and purchase the lands hereinafter described at a price not in excess of a sum equal to the delinquent taxes thereon, interest, penalty and costs provided by law, and the same were stricken off and sold to the said Trustee for the use and benefit of the following funds entitled to the payment of the taxes for which the real estate hereinafter described was sold as follows:

FUNDS			AMOUNT		FUNDS		AMOUNT		
RD & BR	SCHOOL	JR COL	FIRE	CNTY	HEALTH	STATE	HANDI	AMBU
44.50	799.47	91.18	104.84	0.00	18.63	5.92	18.63	27.92
Interest:								
23.26	414.81	47.83	54.66	0.23	9.77	3.06	9.77	14.68

TOTAL $1,871.09

All of which proceedings are shown by deed from the Collector of said County to ████████, Trustee, dated the 1st day of December 2004, and recorded in the Office of the Recorder of Deeds of ████████ County, ████████, in deed record book ████, at page number ████, ████ AND ████; and,

WHEREAS, the said Grantor has been offered the sum of FIVE HUNDRED TWELVE DOLLARS AND SEVENTY-SEVEN CENT ($512.77) by the said HEARTLAND HIDEAWAYS, LLC, a Missouri Corporation Grantee, for the lands hereinafter described; and,

WHEREAS, the County Court, by order of record dated the 6th day of June 2006 has ordered the undersigned to sell the hereinafter described lands to the said Grantee at that price and sum, and to execute and deliver a deed therefor.

NOW, THIS INDENTURE, WITNESSETH, That the said Grantor, under and acting by virtue and in pursuance of the powers in him vested as hereinbefore stated, in consideration of the sum of FIVE HUNDRED TWELVE DOLLARS AND SEVENTY-SEVEN CENT ($512.77), to him in hand paid by the said HEARTLAND HIDEAWAYS, LLC, a Missouri Corporation Grantee, the receipt of which is hereby acknowledged, does by these presents, grant, bargain sell and convey unto the said Grantee, the piece or parcel of land situated in the County of ████████, State of ████████ and described as follows:

██-██-3B-██-009-4██.00
SUR RTS ████████
LOT 4 & 5 BLOCK █

TO HAVE AND TO HOLD the above described premises together with all and singular the hereditaments and appurtenances thereto belonging or in anywise appertaining unto the said Grantee, their heirs and assigns forever.

IN TESTIMONY WHEREOF, the said Grantor has hereunto set his hand this 13th day of June ____.

Trustee/Grantor

STATE OF ____)
) SS
COUNTY OF ____)

Before me, the undersigned, in and for said County, this day, personally came the above-mentioned ____, Trustee, described in the foregoing instrument, and acknowledged that he executed the same for the uses and purposes therein mentioned.

IN WITNESS WHEREOF, I have hereunto set my hand and seal this 13th day of June ____.

Notary Public
State of ____

My Commission Expires: ____
Commissioned in ____ County

Here is a copy of the actual letter report from the title company:

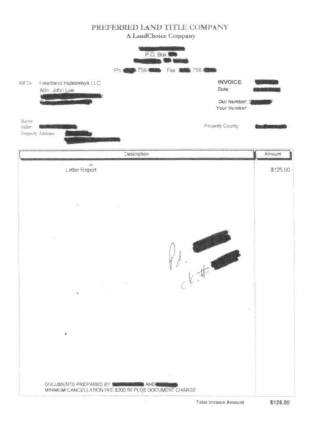

PREFERRED LAND TITLE COMPANY
A LandChoice Company

P.O. BOX
TELEPHONE
EMAIL: @LANDCHOICE.NET

PROVIDING TITLE INSURANCE CLOSINGS AND ESCROW SERVICES IN

June 12,

Heartland Hideaways LLC
John Lee

Dear John:

PREFERRED LAND TITLE COMPANY has examined the records of the office of the Recorder of Deeds for the County of ████████, State of ████████, in regard to the following described Tract of Land situated in the County of ████████, State of ████████, to-wit:

All of the SURFACE RIGHTS ONLY in and to Lots Four (4) and Five (5), Block ████, ████, Town of ████████, as shown on a plat of said town recorded in Plat Book 5 at page 17 of the Land Records of ████████ County, ████████

and hereby certifies that the last owner(s) of record is ████████, Trustee

That we find no Deeds of Trust on record as of the date of this report for this description.

That we find no Requests for Notice under R.S.Mo. 443.325 on record as of the date of this report.

That we find no Federal Tax Liens on record as of the date of this report.

That according to the Tax Records for the County of ████████, County Taxes for the year ████ and prior years are paid.

That according to the Tax Records for the City of ████████, City Taxes for the year ████ and prior years are paid.

There are no Special Taxes.

Subject to right, title or interest of ████████ and ████████, husband and wife, who was the last record owner of the property when it was sold for taxes for the years 1999, 2000 and 2001 by the County of ████████. The Collector's Deed is recorded in Book ████ at page ████.

There are no Judgments, Lis Pendens or Mechanics' Liens abstracted in said office against said owners of Record that are liens thereon.

The liability hereunder is limited to the price of this report.

Dated this **9th** day of **June,** █████ at **8:00 A.M.**

Preferred Land Title Company

By ████████████ President

██████
RAY

Here is a copy of the actual Quiet Title law suit judgment:

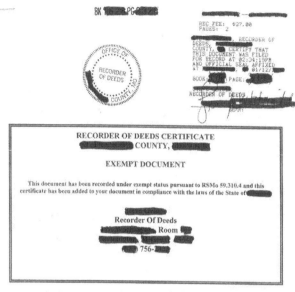

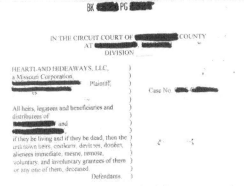

BK ███ PG ███

IN THE CIRCUIT COURT OF ███ COUNTY
AT ███ ███
DIVISION

HEARTLAND HIDEAWAYS, LLC, a Missouri Corporation,	)
Plaintiff,	)
███ vs.	) Case No. ███ ███
All heirs, legatees and beneficiaries and distributees of ███ and ███, if they be living and if they be dead, then the unknown heirs, consorts, devisees, donees, alienees immediate, mesne, remote, voluntary, and involuntary grantees of them or any one of them, deceased.	)
Defendants.	)

JUDGMENT AND DECREE

Now on this 5th day of January, ███, this cause comes on for hearing and Defendants, having been duly served and notified by publication as prescribed by law, and Plaintiff, Heartland Hideaways, LLC, appearing with its Attorney, ███ ███ and the Defendants not present in person, the case is taken up and submitted to the Court upon the pleadings and evidence. The Court being advised in the premises, does approve the service by publication as made upon the aforesaid Defendants, and does further find the issues in favor of the Plaintiff and against the Defendants.

NOW THEREFORE, it is ordered, adjudged and decreed that Plaintiff is vested with the fee simple title in and to the real estate described in the petition to-wit:

All of the SURFACE RIGHTS ONLY in and to Lots Four (4) and Five (5), Block ███ ███, Town of ███, as shown on a plat of said town recorded in Plat Book ███ at page ███ of the Land Records of ███ County, ███.

And it is further ordered, adjudged, found and decreed that Defendants, their heirs, legatees and beneficiaries be forever enjoined and restrained from asserting, claiming or setting up any right, title or interest in and to said real estate or any lien

███ ███

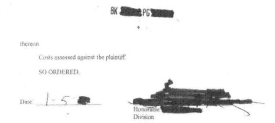

BK ████ PG ███████

thereon.

Costs assessed against the plaintiff.

SO ORDERED.

Date ___1 - 5___ ██

Honorable _____
Division

Here is a copy of proceeds from the title company:

City Lots Sold With a Realtor

In June of one year, I bought four adjoining city lots from the county trustee.

The following is a breakdown of my costs:

County Taxes $171.85

Letter report from the title company	$125.00
Attorney fees for quiet-title lawsuit	$450.00
Court cost for quiet title lawsuit	$130.44
Engineering fee for survey	$700.00
Total Costs	**$1,577.29**

I usually do not have properties surveyed. However, because this property already had all four lots listed on the deed, I thought I might split it up. As it turned out, I did not. Nevertheless, it was money well-spent as the property sold more easily and quickly with the inclusion of a new survey clearly marking the property's boundaries.

One of the things I've learned along the way is that if a deed specifies individual lots, you can easily separate them without engineering work and hassles. It's a great way to increase your profits with tax sale properties. Over the years, I have separated many lots.

On September 26th of that same year, I received a judgment in my favor for the quiet title law suit. I then listed the property with a realtor for $11,900.

I received an immediate offer for $8,500, which I accepted. I received a net check from the title company in the amount of $7,531.16 on October 16th. Maybe I could have gotten a better offer, but it was a quick sale.

Here is a breakdown of how the money flowed:

Check received	$7,531.16
Total costs	$1,617.29
Net profit	**$5,913.87**

I invested about 2 to 3 hours of my time in this deal, counting the time it took me to pick up my check. I also spent about $20 in gasoline and $20 for lunch.

Here is an actual copy of the deed I received from the CountyTrustee:

TRUSTEE'S DEED

Under Collector's Third Tax Sale

THIS INDENTURE, made and entered into this 13th day of June ████, by and between ████████████, GRANTOR herein, for the use and benefit of the funds hereinafter mentioned, and HEARTLAND HIDEAWAYS, LLC a Missouri Corporation, GRANTEE herein, of the County of St. Louis, State of Missouri. Mailing address of grantee is ████████████████, ██████ ██, ████.

LEGAL DESCRIPTION OF THE PROPERTY CONVEYED HEREIN IS SET FORTH ON PAGE 2.

WITNESSETH THAT:

WHEREAS, the County Court of ████████ County, ████████ by an order of record dated the 3rd day of June, 1975, a certified copy of which is on file in the Office of the County Collector of said county, did designate and appoint Grantor as a Trustee for the benefit of all funds entitled to participate in the funds entitled to the taxes against the lands herein described; and,

WHEREAS, the said Grantor has accepted said appointment and is now the duly appointed, qualified and acting Trustee for the uses and purposes aforesaid; and,

WHEREAS, the said Grantor, by virtue aforesaid appointment, is now and was at all the times hereinafter stated authorized to bid at all sales of delinquent lands offered for taxes, interest, penalty and costs, by the collector of said county, which had been offered for sale for taxes for two successive years next prior thereto; and,

WHEREAS, the said Grantor is and was at all the times herein mentioned, authorized to purchase at such sales all lands or lots offered thereat, necessary to protect all taxes due and owing, and to prevent their loss to the taxing authorities involved from inadequate bids; and,

WHEREAS, ████████████, Collector of ████████ County, ██████ did on the 1st day of December 2004 offer for sale for taxes for the third time, the lands hereinafter described, and at said sale no person having bid therefor a sum equal to the delinquent taxes thereon, interest, penalty and the costs provided by law, ████████████, the undersigned Trustee for the uses and purposes herein set forth, and by virtue of the authority vested in him, did bid and purchase the lands hereinafter described at a price not in excess of a sum equal to the delinquent taxes thereon, interest, penalty and costs provided by law, and the same were stricken off and sold to the said Trustee for the use and benefit of the following funds entitled to the payment of the taxes for which the real estate hereinafter described was sold as follows:

FUNDS		AMOUNT		FUNDS		AMOUNT	
RD & BR	SCHOOL	JR COL	CNTY	HEALTH	STATE	HANDI	AMBU
4.82	84.56	9.84	0.00	1.99	0.65	1.99	3.01
Interest:							
2.10	36.44	4.26	0.00	0.87	0.29	0.87	1.32

TOTAL $227.41

All of which proceedings are shown by deed from the Collector of said County to ████████████, Trustee, dated the 1st day of December 2004, and recorded in the Office of the Recorder of Deeds of ████████ County, Missouri, in deed record book ████, at page number ████, ████ and ████; and,

WHEREAS, the said Grantor has been offered the sum of One Hundred one dollars and eighty-five cents ($101.85) by the said HEARTLAND HIDEAWAYS, LLC, a Missouri Corporation Grantee, for the lands hereinafter described; and,

WHEREAS, the County Court, by order of record dated the 6th day of June ████ has ordered the undersigned to sell the hereinafter described lands to the said Grantee at that price and sum, and to execute and deliver a deed therefor.

NOW, THIS INDENTURE, WITNESSETH, That the said Grantor, under and acting by virtue and in pursuance of the powers in him vested as hereinbefore stated, in consideration of the sum of One Hundred one dollars and eighty-five cents ($101.85), to him in hand paid by the said HEARTLAND HIDEAWAYS, LLC, a Missouri Corporation Grantee, the receipt of which is hereby acknowledged, does by these presents, grant, bargain sell and convey unto the said Grantee, the piece or parcel of land situated in the County of ████████, State of ████████ and described as follows:

████-10-12-██-000-████████
SUR RTS ████████
LOTS 12 THRU 15 BLK ██

TO HAVE AND TO HOLD the above described premises together with all and singular the hereditaments and appurtenances thereto belonging or in anywise appertaining unto the said Grantee, their heirs and assigns forever.

IN TESTIMONY WHEREOF, the said Grantor has hereunto set his hand this 13th day of June ■■■.

Trustee/Grantor

STATE OF MISSOURI)
) SS
COUNTY OF ST. FRANCOIS)

Before me, the undersigned, in and for said County, this day, personally came the above-mentioned ■■■■■■, Trustee, described in the foregoing instrument, and acknowledged that he executed the same for the uses and purposes therein mentioned.

IN WITNESS WHEREOF, I have hereunto set my hand and seal this 13th day of June ■■■.

Notary Public
State of Missouri

My Commission Expires: 07-06-■■■
Commissioned in ■■■■ County

  County
My Commission Expires

53

Here is an actual copy of the Title Report from the Title Company:

PREFERRED LAND TITLE COMPANY
A LandChoice Company

P.O. BOX
TELEPHONE   FAX
EMAIL: LANDCHOICE

PROVIDING TITLE INSURANCE CLOSING AND ESCROW SERVICES IN

July 5,

Heartland Hideaways LLC
John Lee

Dear John:

PREFERRED LAND TITLE COMPANY has examined the records of the office of the Recorder of Deeds for the County of   , State of   in regard to the following described Tract of Land situated in the County of   , State of   , to-wit:

All of the SURFACE RIGHTS ONLY in and to Lots Twelve (12), Thirteen (13), Fourteen (14) and Fifteen (15), Block   ( ), Town of   , as shown on a plat thereof, recorded in Plat Book   at page   of the Land Records of   County,

and hereby certifies that the last owner(s) of record is **Heartland Hideaways, LLC a Missouri Corporation**

and that the above described property is subject to:

That we find no Deeds of Trust on record as of the date of this report for this description.

That we find no Requests for Notice under R.S.Mo. 443.325 on record as of the date of this report.

That we find no Federal Tax Liens on record as of the date of this report.

That according to the Tax Records for the County of   , County Taxes for the year   and prior years are paid.

That according to the Tax Records for the City of   , City Taxes for the year   and prior years are paid.

City taxes for   are DELINQUENT.

NOTE: City real estate taxes for the year   are paid.

Form 6770 Dec TITLE Rev. Certified PLTX 63482998

There are no Special Taxes.

Subject to right, title or interest of ████████ and ████████, as Trustees of the █████ Grandchildren Trust, who was the last record owner of the property when it was sold for taxes for the years 1999, 2000 and 2001 by the County of ████████ The Collector's Deed is recorded in Book ███ at page ███

There are no Judgments, Lis Pendens or Mechanics' Liens abstracted in said office against said owners of Record that are liens thereon.

The liability hereunder is limited to the price of this report.

Dated this **28th** day of **June,** ████ at **8:00 A.M.**

Preferred Land Title Company

By ████████ President

████████
RAY

Here are the actual copies of the Engineering order and Survey:

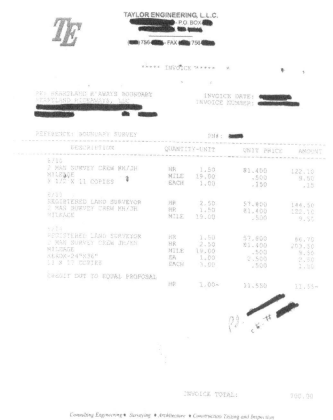

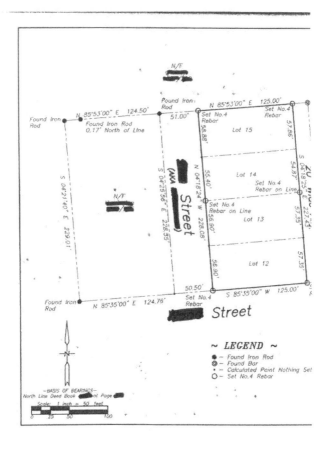

Plat of a Resurvey

Lots 12 thru 15
Block ▆▆, ▆▆▆▆▆▆▆

A subdivision filed for record in Plat Book ▆ at Page ▆
of the Land Records of ▆▆▆▆▆▆▆ County, ▆▆▆▆▆
~ City of ▆▆▆▆▆ ~

THIS IS TO CERTIFY that during the month of August at the request of Heartland Hideaways, L.L.C., I did survey the tracts shown hereon and that the results are shown correctly hereon and described as follows:

Lots 12 thru 15 Block ▆▆, ▆▆▆▆▆▆ a subdivision filed for record in Plat Book ▆ at Page ▆ of the Land Records of ▆▆▆▆▆▆ County, ▆▆▆▆

SUBJECT TO ALL easements, conditions, restictions and right-of-ways of record and those not of record.

I FURTHER DECLARE that under my direct supervision and to the best of my knowledge, information and belief, the results shown hereon are make in accordance with the Current Minimum Standards for a Class (A) URBAN Property Survey of the ▆▆▆▆ Minimum Standards for a Property Boundary Survey.

PLS ▆▆▆▆▆▆

No. 4
bar

TAYLOR ENGINEERING		
P O BOX ▆▆▆▆▆▆ STREET		
Tele: (▆▆)756-▆▆		
Fax ▆▆ 756-▆▆		
Drawn By: ▆▆▆▆	Date: ▆▆▆	File Name: Heartland Hideaways L.L.C.
Approved By: ▆▆▆▆	Scale: 1" = 50'	Project No. ▆▆▆▆

Here are actual copies of the Quiet Title Law Suit
Judgment:

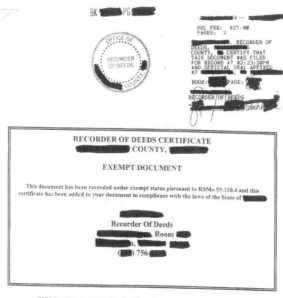

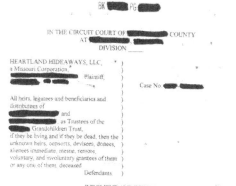

BK ▮▮▮ PG ▮▮▮

IN THE CIRCUIT COURT OF ▮▮▮▮▮ COUNTY
AT ▮▮▮▮▮▮
DIVISION _____

HEARTLAND HIDEAWAYS, LLC,
a Missouri Corporation,)
)
                Plaintiff,)
▮▮▮▮ ▮▮▮   )
                ▮▮▮)   Case No ▮▮▮ ▮▮▮
)
All heirs, legatees and beneficiaries and)
distributees of)
▮▮▮▮▮▮ and)
▮▮▮▮ as Trustees of the)
▮▮▮ Grandchildren Trust,)
if they be living and if they be dead, then the)
unknown heirs, consorts, devisees, donees,)
alienees immediate, mesne, remote,)
voluntary, and involuntary grantees of them)
or any one of them, deceased)
                Defendants.)

JUDGMENT AND DECREE

Now on this 26th day of September, ▮▮▮ this cause comes on for hearing and Defendants, having been duly served and notified by publication as prescribed by law, and Plaintiff, Heartland Hideaways, LLC, appearing with its Attorney, ▮▮▮ ▮ ▮▮▮ and the Defendants not present in person, the case is taken up and submitted to the Court upon the pleadings and evidence. The Court being advised in the premises, does approve the service by publication as made upon the aforesaid Defendants, and does further find the issues in favor of the Plaintiff and against the Defendants.

NOW THEREFORE, it is ordered, adjudged and decreed that Plaintiff is vested with the fee simple title in and to the real estate described in the petition to-wit:

All of the SURFACE RIGHTS ONLY in and to Lots Twelve (12), Thirteen (13), Fourteen (14) and Fifteen (15), Block ▮▮▮ ▮▮ ▮▮, Town of ▮▮▮▮ as shown on a plat thereof, recorded in Plat Book ▮ at page ▮ of the Land Records of ▮▮▮ County, ▮▮▮.

And it is further ordered, adjudged, found and decreed that Defendants, their heirs, legatees and beneficiaries be forever enjoined and restrained from asserting

FILED

▮▮▮▮▮

▮▮▮▮▮ CIRCUIT CLERK
▮▮▮▮

61

BK [redacted] PG [redacted]

claiming or setting up any right, title or interest in and to said real estate or any lien thereon.

Costs assessed against the plaintiff.

SO ORDERED.

Date: *September 24,* [redacted]

[redacted]
Honorable [redacted]
Division [redacted]

STATE OF [redacted]
COUNTY OF [redacted] } ss.

I, [redacted], Clerk of the Circuit Court, in and for said County, hereby certify the above and foregoing to be a true copy of the proceedings of our said Circuit Court, on the day and year above written as the same appears of record in my office.

IN TESTIMONY WHEREOF, I have hereunto set my hand and affixed the seal of said Court in my office in Farmington, Missouri, this *21st* day of *September*, 20[redacted]

[redacted] CIRCUIT CLERK

SEAL BY [redacted]
Deputy Clerk

FILED

SEP 2 6 [redacted]

[redacted], CIRCUIT CLERK
[redacted] COUNTY, [redacted]

Here is a copy of my Proceed check from the Title Company:

Chapter Four

Swift Start on a Shoestring Budget

VISION IS THE ART OF SEEING WHAT IS INVISIBLE TO OTHERS...~JONATHON SWIFT~...

BOUGHT - $91

SOLD - $454

BOUGHT - $426

SOLD - $5600, 75/MONTH - 0% INTEREST

PREVIOUSLY SOLD TWICE — COLLECTED - $1125 + 475 = $1600

Bought – 2 lots - $232 – split double lot

Sold – house - $6900 - $200 down – 75/month – 0% interest

Sold lot - $2400 - $20.50 down – 19/month – 0% interest – he pays $25/month

BOUGHT – 2 HOUSES – 1 COMPLETELY BURNED – 6 ½ LOTS - $546 + 81 = $627 TOTAL

SOLD - $8460 - $75/MONTH – 0% INTEREST

SOLD PREVIOUSLY TWICE – COLLECTED $1100 +1050 = $2150

BOUGHT - $259

SOLD - $2295 - $25/MONTH — 0% INTEREST

BOUGHT 23 LOTS - $1043

SOLD - $50,000 - $200/MONTH – 0%
INTEREST

BOUGHT - 3 LOTS - $138

SOLD - $5500 - $49/MONTH — 0% INTEREST

Bought – 4 lots - $184

Sold - $8900 - $69/month – 0% interest

BOUGHT – 3 LOTS - $ 138

SOLD - $8350 - $77/MONTH – 0% INTEREST

Bought - $46

Sold - $2500 - $22/month — 0% interest

BOUGHT - $46

SOLD - $2400 - $24/MONTH – 0% INTEREST

BOUGHT - $46

SOLD - $2200 - $21/MONTH – 0% INTEREST

BOUGHT - $37

SOLD - $2300 - $23/MONTH — 0% INTEREST

BOUGHT - $145

SOLD - $2844 - $25/MONTH – 0% INTEREST

BOUGHT - $162

SOLD - $1800 - $25/MONTH – 0% INTEREST

BOUGHT - $251

SOLD - $2600 - $29/MONTH – 0% INTEREST

BOUGHT - $259

SOLD - $1464 – CASH

BOUGHT - 2 LOTS - $189 + $58 = $247

SOLD – BOTH TOGETHER - $7150 - $400 DOWN - $79/MONTH – 0% INTEREST

BOUGHT - 2 LOTS - $110 + $179 = $289 TOTAL

SOLD – BOTH LOTS TOGETHER - $5195 - $50 DOWN - $50/MONTH – 0% INTEREST

Bought - $78

Sold - $1229

BOUGHT - $63

SOLD - $680 + $199 CLOSING FEE = $879

BOUGHT - $48

SOLD - $425 + $199 CLOSING FEE = $624 – CHECK

BOUGHT - $78

SOLD - $530.77 + $199 CLOSING FEE = $729.77 – PAYPAL

BOUGHT – 2 LOTS - $63 + $77 = $140

SOLD - $647 + $1059 = $1706

BOUGHT - $63

SOLD - $562.02 + $199 CLOSING FEE = $761.02 – PAYPAL

Bought - $78

Sold - $1000 + $199 closing fee = $1199 – PayPal

BOUGHT - $78

SOLD - $515 + $199 CLOSING FEE = $714 —
PAYPAL

BOUGHT - $84

SOLD - $505

BOUGHT - $99

SOLD - $900 — CASH

BOUGHT - $84

SOLD - $720 –AUCTION

BOUGHT – 5 LOTS - $229 EACH X 5 = $1145

SOLD - $4093 – AUCTION - PAYPAL

Bought - $84

Sold - $682 – auction - PayPal

BOUGHT - $84

SOLD - $809 – AUCTION – PAYPAL

BOUGHT - $349

SOLD - $1006.77 – AUCTION – PAYPAL

BOUGHT – 2 LOTS - $84 + 84 = $168

SOLD - $1828

BOUGHT - $76

SOLD - $195 + $199 CLOSING FEE = $394 - TOTAL

BOUGHT - $106

SOLD - $710 – AUCTION – PAYPAL

BOUGHT - $29

SOLD - $1025 + $145 CLOSING FEE = $1170 - TOTAL

BOUGHT - $91

SOLD - $1025 + $279 CLOSING FEE = $1304

Bought 4 lots - $971 – split

Sold - $859 + $402 + $719 + $620 = $2600

Bought - $102

Sold - $1534

BOUGHT & SOLD 100'S OF PROPERTIES IN THIS AREA

BOUGHT - $180

SOLD - $709

Bought - $91

Sold - $604

Bought - $207

Sold - $1059

BOUGHT – 4 LOTS - $1074

SOLD – SPLIT - $427 + $1199 + $524 + $1109 = $3259

Bought - $79

Sold - $394

BOUGHT - $79

SOLD - $1351

BOUGHT – 2 LOTS - $98

SOLD – SPLIT- $806 + $899 = $1705

BOUGHT - $143

SOLD - $604

BOUGHT - $83

SOLD - $616

Bought & Sold over 600 properties in this area

BOUGHT & SOLD OVER 700 PROPERTIES IN THIS AREA

BOUGHT & SOLD ABOUT 100 PROPERTIES IN THIS AREA

JOHN LEE

Chapter Five

FREE Money...Just for Asking

MONEY WILL COME WHEN YOU ARE DOING THE RIGHT THING...~MIKE PHILLIPS~...

Along the way, I have discovered that many people will actually *give* me their property for *FREE!* Well, not exactly *free* for me, but free to them. They simply sign their properties over to me in exchange for my paying the back taxes that they owe.

How do I manage to do this? First, I contact the county and request of list of properties that have delinquent taxes owed on them. I then contact the property owners and ask them if they are willing to give the properties to me. And, often, they are.

There are certain areas where I prefer to do these kinds of deals. They are places where I am familiar with the region, I know the potential fees that may be involved and I am fairly certain the properties will be easy to sell.

I have come up with a very kind and gentle way of approaching people and asking them to give me their property for what is owed in back taxes.

I send them a letter in which I simply state that I realize that there are many reasons people fall behind on their property taxes. There are deaths, divorces, sometimes people move and sometimes they just do not want to pay them. I then tell them that I would be interested in taking over their responsibility for back and future taxes and that I'm also interested in taking over their future *POA fees* and *special assessments.*

The reason I say *future* POA fees is because I'm not interested in paying hundreds or thousands of dollars in back fees. I know ahead of time what the community will expect because of my due diligence.

I say *future* special assessment fees as well. Special assessments are anything that the community, township, city, county, etc. decides are in the best interest of those involved. This may include fees for such things as sewer laterals, sidewalks, road reconfigurations or any other *improvements* that are beneficial to the community at large.

I conclude the letter by telling the delinquent taxpayer that if my proposal is acceptable to them, they need simply to have the enclosed *general warranty deed* notarized—mentioning that their bank is likely to do this for them at *no* charge as a courtesy—and returned to me in the postage-paid envelope provided. I always include a stamp on the envelope to keep things as easy as possible for the property owners.

On the general warranty deed, I will list my company name as the *grantee*, (i.e. new owner, recipient, etc.) I do not want to take title of the property using my personal name. My company will be selling the property so it should have ownership.

When I send out these letters, however, I always use my *personal* name on both the letter and the envelope. Even my return envelope (SASE) is made out to me personally. I do not hide the fact that my company will be taking possession of their property; I just don't volunteer it.

Why do I do it this way? Mainly because I want my prospects to open the envelope. They do not know who I am (well probably not, anyway). There is a much greater chance that a person will open a letter from an unknown individual than an unknown company.

With all of the *emails, texts, voice mail and clutter* in our lives, we do not get as much regular *snail mail* as we used to, so my letters do tend to grab people's attention. This method seems to work pretty well and is, in my opinion, somewhat less intrusive.

When I receive a notarized deed back from a property owner, I first check it with a quick last-minute due diligence. This usually involves calling the county to verify what I believe I already know.

Provided everything checks out alright, I verify the exact amount of the delinquent taxes that must be brought up to date. I also verify the cost of the filing fees to get the deed recorded.

I mail the deed and recording fee to the *recorder of deeds* (they are sometimes called by different titles, such as *registrar*, depending on the county, so be sure to look that up before sending it).

The payment for the delinquent taxes gets sent separately to the *collector of revenue*. I send these payments separately to avoid confusion. I always want to make everything as easy as possible for the people involved. The last thing I want is for anyone who works for the county to think that I am causing a commotion.

I prefer to be liked. I want to be known as someone who has helped the county, community, town, POA, etc. by bringing money back into the area.

Once I have paid the delinquent taxes and the fees necessary to get the deed recorded, the property is in my name and belongs to me.

How many of my prospects will simply deed their property over to me? It seems to be about 10%. One time, I sent out 40 letters and received three notarized deeds. Another time, I sent out 34 letters and got back four deeds. Most recently, I sent out 22 requests and got back two.

I invariably get a few calls shortly after the letters are sent. Some recipients call because they have questions about my proposal, some call to tell me their stories about why they are delinquent on their payments, and still others call simply to verify that I'm a real person.

Many times, I receive cute little notes and *thank you cards.* This makes me feel good as it verifies that my business venture is also providing a good service to some people. Because of our transaction, their name is cleared from the *tax lien*.

How long does it take me to prepare the letters and deeds? It usually takes me a full afternoon to create around 25 letters of request. I personalize each letter and address each envelope by hand.

I must also prepare each deed individually using the appropriate property and owner information. I send the letter, deed and a self-addressed stamped envelope with each request. So, basically, it costs me the price of a sheet of paper and two stamps per request.

Is it worth the time and the minimal cost that is involved to put all of this together? *Yes.* It is always a good day when someone wants to *give* me their property for *free.*

Chapter Six

The *Sewer Bill* that Came with a *House!*

A GOOD FLUSH BEATS A FULL HOUSE EVERY TIME...~UNKNOWN~...

One day I received a sewer bill in the mail. This was nothing out of the ordinary as I receive lots of sewer bills. I put it in the pile of bills to be paid and forgot about it. A few days later when I was paying the bills, I noticed that something wasn't right.

I did not recognize the address associated with the bill as belonging to one of my properties. I double checked to see if the bill was actually addressed to my company. Sometimes the post cards will stick together and go to a different address.

However, the bill was indeed addressed to me. What the heck was this? I do own a few houses and vacant properties in that vicinity, but none with this address. Or so I thought.

I started going through my files. It didn't take long to rule out the houses I owned in the area—their addresses were certain and did not match the one on the bill. Next I looked through my records of the vacant properties that I was selling off on a monthly basis. Nothing there either.

Finally, I went to the county's website. There I connected the address with a lot number. Upon further research, I discovered that the lot was listed with me as the owner. I was still confused.

I went back through my files and records, and finally figured out the parcel. It was a piece of property that had come with two lots listed on the deed that I received.

Oftentimes, properties generate a lot more profit when you divide them. And that is just what I had done in this case. I had split the parcel into two lots and sold them separately. However, I didn't recall any houses being on either lot.

According to my records, I had bought this particular property from the county about a year and a half earlier. I knew I had gone to the property to see it and take some pictures at the time, as that is my standard operating procedure.

My records showed that I had bought several other properties at the same time that I bought the one in question. Thinking back, I had visited and taken pictures of all my new properties on that particular day.

So, I fired up the computer and looked through my pictures of the property. Nothing looked unusual at all. The property was wooded and covered with growth and vegetation. It looked like all of the other vacant properties that I had photographed that day.

I had originally paid $232 for the double lot. Within a short time of me buying them, each lot sold for $2,400. I sold them at 0% interest on a payment schedule of $25 per month.

I then checked on the status of each of the properties. One buyer had been making consistent payments for the last year and a half and everything was up to date.

The other lot, however, had been given back to me by the buyer after about nine months' worth of payments. It had just been sitting there waiting for me to resell it all this time.

But what could this possibly have to do with the sewer bill?

I assumed the city had simply made a mistake in their billing. These things do happen from time to time. No big deal. I wrote a note on the bill saying there was no sewer line hooked up to this property and sent it back to them.

I figured they would check their records, correct the error, and that would be the end of it. Not so. I got another bill the next month with a new charge and a *late fee*.

I was certain that there was no sewer hooked up to that property. The city thought otherwise. They kept sending bills, and I kept ignoring them.

Eventually, the bill grew to over $190, with the city still insisting they were right. I decided it was time to resolve this situation.

Since it was high time I sold this lot anyway, I planned a day to go and visit my property. I figured I could take some updated pictures of the lot in question and present them to the city as I argued my case.

I grabbed my plat maps and hopped into my truck. The property was located about a two-hour drive from my house. The Ozark Mountains, lakes, streams, forest, and ample wildlife along the way, made for a very scenic drive.

I find lovely drives like this to be very therapeutic. They give me time to think and to listen to the educational audio recordings of some of my mentors.

I was very relaxed by the time I arrived at the street that leads to the property. As I approached it, I didn't notice anything significantly different from the last time I had been here. There were still lots of trees and lots of undergrowth.

When I arrived, I got out of my truck for a closer look. This was the first time I had actually walked on this land since I had bought it. Behind a copse of trees, I spotted some type of structure—a shed, perhaps?

As I made my way forward, I was surprised to discover that it was actually a small house! That's right. Behind the trees there was a house. My first thought was that it was probably okay to go inside and take a look since it was on my property.

Or was it?

Remember, I had split the property up by lots when I'd sold it. One buyer was paying for his property and the other had given his lot back. Was this house located on the lot I *owned outright* or was it on the lot that was currently being paid for?

Either way, there was a sewer bill that was due. And now I could see that it was not an erroneous one. I immediately drove down to city hall and paid the almost two hundred dollars that was owed. I always want to be on good terms with the city.

With the sewer bill up-to-date, I returned to the little house to check it out.

It was a disaster. It appeared to have been ransacked and stuff was all torn up. The carpets were ripped, the walls were caving in, and everything was a complete mess. It was *great*! These are my favorite kinds of houses. Total wrecks.

But the question remained: Did *I* own this property? I couldn't get back home fast enough to find out.

To my elation, I discovered that the house was indeed located on the lot that had been returned to me. The buyer who was still paying each month was putting the money toward the lot next door.

Wow! I had bought a house almost two years earlier that I never even knew I owned. So what was my next move? I put it up for sale, of course! The last thing I wanted was another sewer bill—especially a sewer bill that wasn't being paid for by someone else through rent or property payments.

I quickly wrote up an ad and listed the property on *Craigslist*. It sold in less than a week. Here is the exact wording of my actual ad:

$5900 Fixer Upper Close to the Lake Owner Financing Available (Big Mountain Lake)

XXX Louis Drive

XXX Louis Dr.,Property 200 x 50 feet approximately, has run down house ~ A REAL Fixer-Upper!

$5900 cash or will finance $6900, 69/month (plus 25/month sewer), 0% interest, NO Credit Check !!!

Electric, Sewer, Water available.

Nestled in the Heart of the Ozarks in Beautiful Saint Francois County Located at Big Mountain Lake. This Property is Very Spacious Measuring approximately two hundred feet by fifty feet by two hundred feet by fifty feet (200 x 50 x 200 x 50). Your Property is just a Very Short Walk from Iron Mountain Lake Which Provides Great Fishing for Bass, Crappie, Bluegill and Catfish!

Big Mountain Lake has its Own Police Department and City Hall. The Fire Department is Located in Blackville, just a Short Distance Away. The Close Medical Facilities are in Farrington which is Less than 15 Miles Away. School District is Blackville.

This Property Sets Very Well. The Area is Nicely Treed with Many Hardwoods Including Oaks. Water is Available from Perry Knock Rural Water. Sewer is from Big Mountain Lake. Electric is by American UE. No Tent or Fifth Wheel Camping is Permitted.

There are No Fees or Back Taxes Due. Taxes are Less than two hundred and twenty dollars per year And are Current. Also, There are No Association Fees or Maintenance Fees. This Property is Very Inexpensive to Buy And Very Inexpensive to Keep!

Your Property is Very Close to the National Forest Where You Can Enjoy Some of the Best Hiking and Hunting in the Country. Deer and Turkey are Very Plentiful in the Region.

For You History Buffs, it's Less than 15 Miles to Historic Arondiac Valley Where the Famous Civil War Battle at Fort David Took Place. Tour the Museum And Observe the Cannon Ball Scars on the Buildings. At Certain Times You May View Full Uniform Reenactments of the Actual Battle. Another Interesting Historical Area is Nearby Cherokee Pass Where the InFamous' Trail of Tears'ï¿½ Came Through.

You're Also Very Close to Many Beautiful State Parks.

For You Geology Enthusiasts, You Can Explore the Abandoned Community and Closed Mine at Golden River Mines Recreation Area. At One Time a Thriving Mining Community Operated There. You Can Still Find Traces of Silver, Fools Gold and Many Other Minerals ~ Unusual for the Area. The National Parks Brochure Even Mentions Traces of GOLD Being Found on the Site. They Also Have White Water Kayaking Here at Certain Times of the Year. Kayakers From All Over Attend.

This is a Nice property at a Nice price! Very Inexpensive to Own And Very Inexpensive to keep!

The Pictures We Took on a Recent Visit. This is a Good Value Property. Whether You are Wanting to Enjoy Your Property Now or Just Preparing for Your

135

Future This Is a Great Buy. Get Your Piece of the Heartland While You Still Can. You May Never Again Have the Opportunity to Own Part of the American Dream at Such a GREAT PRICE!!!

Email XXXXXXX @ yahoo . com or Call 314 . XXX . XXXX for More Info .

Thanks for Looking !!!
THINK...EXPLORE...INVEST...
NOW

Of course, I included several pictures of how bad the property looked. I love selling these little *real* fixer-uppers. I could have sold this house about a dozen times!

I also love being able to provide owner financing on these venture properties. People seem to like being able to make small monthly payments to me while taking on a project for themselves. It really works out well for both of us.

The new buyer was very excited about getting the house. She told me that, a couple years earlier, she had bought another dilapidated property through an owner-financing deal offered by someone else. She'd made the necessary home-improvements and paid the property off early.

She now had a renter living in the property and was looking for her next project. She was well aware of what she was getting into as far as repairs were concerned. This house needed everything.

We agreed on a sales price of $6,900 with a $200 down-payment. We also agreed that she would make payments of $75 a month at 0% interest and that she would cover the sewer bill each month as well.

And that's the story of *the sewer bill that came with a house.*

Here is a picture of the house:

Here is a picture of the lot:

Here is a copy of the *Sewer Bill* that came with the house:

Chapter Seven

How to Become the Bank

BANK PROFITS HIT ALL TIME HIGH! ON WEDNESDAY, THE FEDERAL DEPOSIT INSURANCE CORPORATION SAID PROFITS AT US LENDERS HIT AN ALL-TIME HIGH IN 2013. FOR THE YEAR, THE NATIONS BANKS MADE A COLLECTIVE $155 BILLION. THAT'S UP 10% FROM A YEAR AGO AND IT WAS MORE THAN THE $148 BILLION THE BANKS MADE IN 2006, THE LAST TIME PROFITS PEAKED...BY...~STEPHEN GANDEL~...SENIOR EDITOR – CNN MONEY – FEBRUARY 26, 2014 -

A few years ago I started my *own bank.* I provide owner financing for many of my properties. This is something that has always appealed to me. The sound of *being the bank* is a pretty good sound.

I attended a *Russ Whitney Real Estate Seminar* several years ago. The lead trainer was *David Gilmore* (and no, it's not the same David Gilmore from the rock band *Pink Floyd*—although he did play the song "Money" during one of the breaks.) He is a great presenter and an even better real estate investor.

141

This was one of those seminars that really humbled me. At this point in my career, I had been a mortgage broker for several years. I was on my high horse and *thought* I knew quite a bit.

Well, in all fairness, I did have a decent amount of experience from working with investors, oodles of first time homebuyers and people who were working toward rebuilding their credit. The ones that were credit impaired also wanted to buy houses.

I could put a deal together fairly well. Most of my clients came to me through word-of-mouth. In those days, not too many brokers were taking the time to work with those who could not get a loan easily. This was back in the hay-day when lenders were giving out loans like they were candy.

For someone to *not* be able to get a loan back then, they had to be in pretty bad shape credit-wise. That type of person was my typical client. Some were bankrupt or foreclosed on; some were jobless or divorced; some were even homeless or living in hotels. There were all kinds of reasons these people could not qualify for a loan.

There was certainly no lack of this sort of clientele in those days. There are even more people in financial straits today. This is hardly surprising, what with all of the lay-offs, downsizing, transferring of jobs to other countries and, oh yeah, the real estate collapse.

Anyway, I was at this seminar with instructor David Gilmore. He had been in the real estate business for quite a few years and he showed us all kinds of strategies that were non-traditional, i.e. *outside of the box.*

This really resonated with me. Of all the real estate deals I had put together, more than 80 percent fell outside the scope of what would be considered *"normal."* Very rarely did my clients have any money, let alone 20-percent to put down. This doesn't even take into consideration the closing costs, inspections, insurance and all of the other expenses normally associated with buying a home.

In his presentation, David was talking about lease options. This can be a great way for a seller to sell their house or property to someone who may not qualify for a traditional loan. A lease option is similar to seller financing in that the seller still has a major ownership position in the property.

I will not be going into lease options in this book. There is, however, a lot of good information available through books, seminars and other sources if this is something that you think you may want to learn more about.

David did a great job explaining how he took the lease option concept and turned it into owner financing. That was it. I knew at that moment that I needed to become the bank.

I had to put that idea on hold, however.

At the time, I was busily selling about 10 to 15 properties a week on auction sites like eBay. The little properties that I dealt with in those days were selling like hot cakes. I didn't even have time to put them on my website before they were sold and I was out buying more.

This was a fun time in real estate. People were making money hand over fist. No one could do a bad deal. *Everyone* was a real estate investor—or so many of them thought.

By the time 2007 rolled around, many of these *newfound investors* were being taught to depend on appreciation as their way of making their fortune in real estate.

This was a very interesting time. The ratings companies were giving the *packaged loans* from Wall Street fraudulent ratings. They were giving "A" ratings to loan packages that should have been "C" rated or less. These were then sold globally as *secured* investments.

There was so much money coming in from all over the world. Everyone was making money from their *investments* and real estate was appreciating at historical levels.

I knew a lot of people around the country who had accumulated several properties. Many of these investors were banking on appreciation as their business plan. This plan worked well for several years.

Then the bottom fell out.

The *secured* investments went south and plummeted, and the real estate values went with them. At this point, many investors were in a position where not only were they losing equity; they needed more money just to stay in the game.

This time period took all of the *amateurs* out of the mix. Just about everyone who did not have a good business plan went under.

It reminded me of the old *pyramid schemes* or the *Ponzi schemes.* As long as there is new money coming in, everything is great. As soon as there are no new investors, everything comes crashing down.

The crash turned out to be the biggest in history. I don't think there is anyone on earth who was not affected in one way or another.

The mechanics behind the crash are very deep and somewhat complicated. If you would like to know more about what really happened, I would recommend a very informative program put together by CNBC called *House of Cards* (not to be confused with the BBC or Netflix series of the same name). In it, CNBC does a very good job of explaining to us *lay persons* the situations that led to the crash.

Right about the time that all this was going on, my sales on the auction sites started slipping. At first, I experienced problems with several *high bid* auction winners who did not pay. This was frustrating. It costs a lot of money to list and sell real estate on these sites.

At the same time, eBay changed its rules to state that the real-estate auctions were *not* binding and that you were instead entering into a contract to negotiate!

What? Were they crazy? In a word, yes, they were (and are).

I lost several thousand dollars. At first I saw it as a fluke and didn't think too much about it. Then I started seeing property values all around the country going down.

I particularly noticed Florida. I have some friends in that state and like to go there several times a year, including the holidays. I saw one of my friend's building-lots go from more than $150,000 in value to a mere $20,000—and then to less than $5,000! I was thinking "What a great time to buy low-priced properties in Florida!" The problem was that the banks were not loaning money for these properties.

The properties I owned were getting harder and harder to sell. Their selling-prices crashed just like everything else. It was starting to cost me more to buy the properties and resell them (when I finally did sell them) than I was paying for them.

Losing money like this is *not* good business. It was also not any fun and could not continue. At the time, however, I had some major personal things going on in my life so I just left things alone.

Then a realtor friend of mine contacted me about a property I had listed with her less than a week earlier. This particular property was close to a lake and sat on about one and a half acres of land. It had a double-wide mobile home on it as well as a three room cabin with a nice stone fireplace.

It wasn't an expensive property. We had it listed for $19,900; and since I had only invested around $2,000 into it, counting acquisition and repair costs, I figured I would be okay with whatever the sales price turned out to be.

My realtor told me I'd gotten an offer for the full asking price, provided I would be willing to hold the note. The buyer's offer got my attention. I contacted him and asked, "What do you have in mind?"

He said that he would pay two-thousand dollars down and make payments of $300 per month until the property was paid off. We ended up agreeing on him paying the realtor's commission and he said that he would start making payments to me in about six weeks. We also agreed on a 6-percent interest rate on the financing.

We met at the title company. My attorney drew up a *contract for deed.* Everyone was happy: the realtor got her money; the new buyer got to buy the property on terms that were favorable to him; and I got a note for $300 a month for a few years. Sweet!

So that's how I got into the *banking business*. I started receiving checks each month and really liked it. I still do. Why not get my money over time?

I thought back to my training with David Gilmore. I was going to become the bank! *My bank!* I loved the sound of it. Why shouldn't I be the bank? After all, I'm a little nicer and better-looking than *Wells Fargo.*

How would I do this? I decided to change my strategy for buying and selling properties. Instead of selling them right away, I would sell them over time.

When I sold properties through the auction sites, I would usually get my full payment within a week or two. What I planned to do now was totally different. I had to think like a bank. The money would be coming in over a period of *years* instead of *days*.

Back in the old days, I would buy a property for, say, $300. I would typically have some costs involved with the selling, recording and paperwork for the property at a total of around $100. My properties usually sold for cash for anywhere from $700 to $2500.

I made a good profit most of the time. However, because of the way the rules for the auctions had changed and because of the recent real estate collapse, this method was not working for me anymore.

I completely changed the way that I marketed my properties. Rather than rely on the auction sites, I switched to the *classified* and *fixed-price* type sites.

The method I came up involved advertising the properties as follows:

Low down payment, low monthly payments, 0% interest, No credit check.

You might be thinking, "What? Are you crazy?" Well, maybe. Clearly, however, this has become a good model for me. An example of how this works can be seen the following real-life scenarios:

Example One:

I bought a property from the county for $145.71, plus about $100 in various fees. I ran an ad for a down-payment auction on eBay. I spent about $80 for the listing. So my total costs were around $350.

The terms of my auction were that the buyer would remit the bid-on down-payment plus a $199 closing fee within seven days of end-of-auction. The total contract price of the property was $3,190, minus the down payment. The monthly payments were set at $25 at 0% interest, until paid. No credit check was involved.

The high bidder's offer was $52. So he immediately paid me $251. I sent him the property maps and two copies of the sales agreement (contract). He signed one of the copies and returned it in the postage paid envelope I had enclosed for his convenience.

I *always* include a SASE (self-addressed stamped envelope). For those who send in their payments by *regular* mail, I return another SASE each month when I send their receipts. I like to make it very convenient for people to pay me.

In this instance, I had less than $400 invested in the property. I got $250 up front and it took me another six months to get back my original investment. I am also getting a monthly payment of $25 for a total of 125 months.

After the first six months, the $25 payments are *all profit*. That's a total profit of about $2,800. Well, it does require me to give up about five minutes of my time, two postage stamps, two envelopes, a receipt and two photocopies each month—I'd say that's worth it.

I always offer a 10% discount for paying the property off at any time. There is no prepayment penalty. Many people choose to exercise this option whether for tax reasons or just to get the property paid off.

Example Two:

Another property deal that I financed went like this:

I bought a completely run-down house that had been empty for several years. I paid the county $573.08 for the back taxes plus another $70 in fees.

This house was situated on a one-acre lot high on a hill. It overlooked some railroad tracks below and was at the end of a dead-end street. It was a in a very private location, and that was something to be concerned about. Vandals and kids always seem to find the empty houses that are well-hidden as they apparently make for a good place to party.

The house was in very poor shape by the time I bought it. At first I thought I would fix it up. In decent condition, it could easily be rented for around $600 a month. Alternatively, it could be repaired and then resold for more than $50,000.

I figured repair costs would run about $20,000, not counting the *unknown factor* (this is all of the unexpected, necessary repairs that I would inevitably run into.) I like to figure in another 20 to 25 percent for unknowns when calculating my expected costs.

Either way, the deal seemed to make sense. I could make some money on a quick sale or I could have some long term cash flow by renting it. I had several other projects going on at the time, however, so this one got moved to the back burner for a while.

Around this time, the hard-drive on my computer crashed. I lost more than 10-years' worth of photos! I found out that this is the downside of digital photos. Losing them to a computer crash is similar to having your printed photos burn up in a fire.

Once your photos are gone, they're gone. Sure, I attempted to have them recovered. I called around and let some professionals work on it. They said they could get my files back for me. A couple of weeks and more than $500 later, I still had no photos.

By this time, I had moved a few of my priorities around and decided I wanted to sell the house as-is rather than fix it up.

Repairing the house, which was located about 35 miles from my home, would have been a major undertaking and the $20,000+ needed would have come out of my pocket. Selling the place as-is just seemed the best option for me at that time.

I was preparing to list it when I realized I no longer had any photos. No biggie. I could just drive out and get some new ones. My old ones were a little dated anyway. It had been several months since I had even seen the place.

Going out to look at a house that I own—especially when I haven't seen it in a while—can seem like Christmas. New toys...all over again! I was looking forward to seeing the place.

When I got there, though, my jaw hit the ground. The house was in bad shape when I bought it. Now it was in really, *really* bad shape.

In the several months since I'd last seen it, the home had had some more visitors. The *metal thieves* had shown up. They almost always find the empty houses.

It doesn't really matter if the homes are in the city or in the country. The metal thieves seem to be attracted like magnets.

There was also much more damage. The vandals had torn up the walls to get to the wires and pipes. They'd done a heck of a demolition job on the house. The shed and car-port were further damaged as well. And on top of all that, the roof was falling in. It was a real mess.

I was glad that my hard-drive crash had forced to go get new photos. This property was very different than it was a few months ago. Necessary repairs to this property would be far more expensive than originally anticipated.

I listed the property in a free ad on Craigslist. It was a small ad for a *"Real Fixer Upper"* that needed everything. The ad went something like this:

"Handy Man Special – A Real Fixer Upper – Only $5900 cash or Possible Owner Financing – Low Down Payment – 0% Interest – No Credit Check – ONLY $50 per month for total of $6500 – Call for details."

I got some phone calls of inquiry in the first few days. A couple of people offered to take it sight-unseen. This invariably happens. I always tell these prospective buyers to go look at it first, and then we'll talk.

One of the two people who expressed an interest in the house did go and look at the property. He called the next day and said that he definitely wanted it. After verifying that he did indeed go see it, I set up time to meet.

We met and agreed on a sales price of $6,500. He gave me $200 down and we agreed on payments of $50 a month—this comes to more than 10 years of payments—at 0% interest until paid in full.

He said he would likely pay more each month. In the years since we made this deal, there have actually only been two months in which he paid only the $50 minimum. He almost always pays $75 or $100 each month.

This buyer planned to fix up the house. He is a laid off construction worker who has some good basic skills. He was looking for a weekend project that could also make him some money.

One of the things that I learned from this buyer is that you can actually get building materials for free. He combs the Craigslist ads every day looking for what he needs. While doing his temporary delivery job, he drives his little truck all over town and gets *free* building materials.

There are all kinds of things on Craigslist in the *Free Section*. When people are done with their home projects, they usually do not need the left-over material and often find giving it away easier than disposing of it.

My buyer has been working on the house for about two and a half years now and has hardly spent any money on supplies. While he has to look through the ads and drive to the places to pick up the materials, it's a good, solid plan.

Total numbers for this deal:

The original cost for me was about $650. My advertising cost was $0. I received $200 down and an expectation of at least $50 in payments each month. With minimum payments only, my full costs would have been reimbursed in the first nine months. Because my buyer makes larger monthly payments, I actually got my full investment back in about four months.

Our original agreement would have gone for 126 months (10.5 years) at $50 per month. As it turns out, he should have this home paid off in about five or six years.

He is fixing the house up really nicely. He should come out pretty well and make some good money with it.

I am also coming out pretty well. I am making about $5,800 in profit. Sure, I could have made more. This deal just made the most sense at the time. Also, as I said before, I love getting payments in the mail each month.

Again, this deal takes me about five minutes of time and paperwork each month.

Example Three:

Throughout the years, I have had many buyers acquire multiple properties. In the early days I sold them all for cash. Over the last few years I have financed most of them.

Here is a typical multiple-property deal that I recently financed:

I bought two lots from the county for $36.13 each. I bought a third lot for $75.46. These purchases came with additional fees of $15 for each. My total investment was therefore $192.72.

I ran an ad on eBay that cost me $80, bringing my total investment to just under $300. One buyer bought all three lots.

We agreed on a $504 down payment and a total sales price of $8,350 for the three lots combined. My buyer's payments are $77 per month at 0% interest until paid in full. As usual, there was no credit check involved.

With the down-payment, my initial investment of about $300 was recouped immediately with a profit of about $200. In addition, I will be receiving $77 a month for 101 months (8.4 years). My total profit on this deal is almost $8,000!

I have done many deals like this over the years. It's a different way of doing business that provides a win~win~win scenario for everyone involved.

The county gets their money from the delinquent taxes and can also count on getting their current and future tax dollars for the property. The buyer is happy because he bought a low-cost piece of property at a good price and with great terms.

I am also very happy because I get a nice monthly income for many years to come. I have many agreements like this one that vary quite a bit in terms and amounts.

Cash-Flow Is King

The smallest notes I finance are $25 per month. The largest ones I have are for more than $500. These notes can range in terms from about 2-½ years to more than 25 years.

I used to hear the saying, "Cash is king." Today, I believe that *Cash **Flow** is King!* I love to receive monthly payments. You may not get too excited about the thought of $25 per month. What if you have a hundred such payments coming in? What if you have five hundred?

With five hundred accounts at $25 per month, that comes to $12,500 in monthly income. If you spend five minutes on each deal each month, this will come to a total of about 42 hours a month in labor. Don't have the time? Pay someone $15 an hour to do it for you. Forty-two hours of work will cost you $630, still leaving you with a profit of almost $12,000 each month.

Besides accepting checks, I also accept PayPal™ for credit cards and e-checks. They charge about 3.1% for their services. At first I thought it was a little expensive as they used to charge 2.75%.

This is actually is pretty reasonable rate considering the service they provide. A lot of people are very secure with using PayPal. They are a reliable third-party that validates all parties involved by our bank accounts. They have guarantees and provide ways to get your money back in the case of a fraudulent transaction.

There are only a couple minor things that I have to do a little differently when someone pays by PayPal. I still create a receipt for them each month, but I send it by email instead of regular mail. There are no stamps or envelopes involved. I then simply print out a copy of their PayPal transaction and a copy of their receipt for my files. It's quick and easy.

Most of my buyers still use the good old-fashioned USPS to send me checks through snail mail. I love having a mailbox that brings me money.

My process is very easy. When I receive a payment, I pull out the customer's file. I prepare a receipt and print it. I then copy the receipt along with their check for my files.

I prepare and print two envelopes. One envelope is addressed to the buyer. One is an SASE back to me. Yes, I do put a stamp on the return envelope and pay for the postage.

I also keep the envelope they returned to me with their payment (the one I sent to them the previous month). This shows me how long it takes their check to get to me from wherever they live. It is also a good thing to have if I ever need to put together a record of their payment history. Many times these are needed for a traditional bank loan.

My paperwork is very simple. I am happy to share it with you. Here it is:

Here is a copy of my Contract for Deed, or my *Agreement*:

Contract For Deed

This agreement constitutes a purchase of the property below by the undersigned:

TIMBERWOLF MOUNTAIN
LOT 2957 Red Oak Drive
Belmount MO

The following provisions and stipulations are a part of this agreement:

Sales price is **$ 13661** . *Purchaser will pay a nonrefundable down payment of* **$ 950** *and Monthly payments of* **$239** *at* **0%.**
Payments are due on the **18th** *of each month beginning* **APRIL 18** , **2013**

Upon satisfactory repayment the seller will execute and deliver unto the purchaser a special warranty deed conveying title in fee simple to the subject property.

In the event all agreed payments are not paid in a timely manner, i.e. three months in arrears, then the purchasers forfeit all claims to the subject property. The seller may re-enter and take full possession of the subject property. Checks returned from your bank for any reason will result in an additional $39 charge. This property may be paid in full at any time with no prepayment penalty.

In the event purchaser can obtain other financing, upon receipt of the payoff funds, the seller will execute and deliver unto the purchaser a special warranty deed conveying title in fee simple to the subject property.

Taxes and Insurance are to be paid by the purchaser.

Purchaser   *John Doe* _____   *Date* _____

Purchaser   *Jane Doe* _____   *Date* _____

Seller Heartland Hideaways LLC _____   *Date* _____
Member of the Management Team John Lee

Here is a sample copy of the receipt that I send to my buyers each month:

March 25, 2013

Received from ____ Ben & Kristi Wilson

For payment: check/mo/cash/paypal/echeck of **$50**

Property address: L7 P8 Sec 11 Silver Springs, Cheyenne IL

Any balance due $4542.11*

Next regular investment of **$50** is due on **05/20/2013~**

~Investments made before &/or in addition to regular
Investments, will be applied 100% to principal~

Please Allow Time for mailing.

Thank you,

John Lee
Management Team

Heartland RE Investments LLC
12345 Main Street
AwesomeTown USA 12345-6789
123-456-7890
GREinv@yaboo.com

*We will still honor *your* 10% discount when you choose to make the full investment
Now~No Pre-payment penalty!*

Here is a copy of the envelope that I send to my buyers:

Here's a copy of my SASE:

Chapter Eight

Pitfalls to Avoid

IT IS BETTER TO KNOW SOME OF THE QUESTIONS THAN ALL OF THE ANSWERS...~JAMES THURBER~...

Due Diligence*: (n) The investigation or audit of a potential investment.* As part of performing due diligence, I always find out as much as I can about the communities in which the properties I am interested in are located. I also learn as much as I can about their handling of tax liens.

Many people are out there today selling tax-lien and tax-certificate programs. I've seen several of them say that the county tax lien goes to the first position and that all the other liens that may be associated with a property are subordinate and will be *wiped out* when the taxes are paid.

In actuality, the *subordinate liens* (such as mortgage liens) may or may not be wiped out. I have found that most of the time, those who have placed a subordinate lien on a property usually do not care enough to go after their money. If they did care, they would simply have paid the taxes!

Why wouldn't a large bank secure a $50,000 lien on a property by simply paying $500 in back taxes? There are many, many reasons. Today, they have might have bigger fish to fry.

With all the foreclosures, short sales and all the other craziness going on with real estate right now, it is not too surprising. This fact still does not guarantee that you will have a free and clear title. It also does not guarantee that someone will not come after the property later on down the road.

The *association fees* are of major concern with a lot of properties. I have never seen a property that was up for sale for back taxes that was also up-to-date on its association fees. The association will typically put a lien on the property to ensure their interest.

Some associations will not waive the back association fees, period. This makes absolutely no sense to me. If someone owes a couple thousand dollars in back fees and does not pay it, the association gets zero dollars. Chances are good they will continue to get zero dollars well into the future.

When the association is willing to *forgive* the back association-fees, however, there is a better chance that the property will be acquired by new owners. The association can then reasonably expect that they will be paid future association fees by these new owners.

I have met with members of the Boards of Trustees for several associations. Most are very friendly people that care a lot about their communities. They become members of the board so that they can better their neighborhoods. However, they are sometimes met with a lot of opposition and have a hard time making changes.

There appears to be a high turnover-rate for board members. It seems that many go into the position with a lot of good intentions only to find that a lot of residents have a hard time accepting any kind of change. This makes their efforts to improve the community difficult.

When I meet with board members, I am coming in with *good news*. All they have to do is forget about the money that the last, *bad* property owner owes to

169

them, and let the new, *good* property owner start contributing to the coffers again.

This is to their advantage as I have found that any time more money starts coming in, it looks good for the members of the board. I always want to have as many friends on the board of trustees as possible.

It also makes me feel pretty good to know that I am contributing to the community. I like going into neighborhoods, seeing newly erected new street signs or road improvements, etc. and thinking that I may have had a small part in the financing.

There have been many board members over the years that have been on my "Christmas Cookie List." Board members are, after all, just regular people like you and me. They like many of the same things we do—such as cookies. ☺

I have found that a lot of board members are treated like, and often looked upon, as though they were *property inspectors.* Some are met with opposition from the outset. People assume that they don't want to get along. The truth is that most board members really do want to help the community and are simply enforcing the rules.

The associations, whether they are referred to as *Homeowners Associations* (HOA's)*, Property Owners Associations* (POA's) or by any other name, are put in place to keep the community up to a certain standard. Board members are expected to keep things running smoothly and make sure that property owners in the community keep their properties up-to-par.

I have found that I can never have too many friends in the HOA's. There have been many times when these people have been on my side when situations arose and I needed a *friend*. The bottom line is that I am nice to all of them, and it has paid off several times.

Fire tags are another type of lien that will come up now and then. A fire tag is an amount of money that is charged each year to pay for residents' fire protection in the unlikely event of a fire.

Oftentimes, there simply is not enough revenue in the county taxes to pay for everyone to have public fire protection. To make up for this shortfall, many areas are divided into fire districts. These districts are usually protected by *volunteer fire departments*. The money to run these departments comes from the revenue generated by fire tags.

In years past, when you paid your fire tag, you actually got a *tag*. You would display this tag in a spot where the firefighters could see it when they responded to a fire. If they did not see a tag on display, they would watch your place burn.

As you might imagine, this caused a lot of problems and confusion. There were several instances in which people had actually paid for their fire tag, but the tag was just not seen by the firefighters and the place was allowed to burn down. This in turn led to many law suits. It wasn't a very good way keep track of who had paid and who hadn't.

Today they don't give you a physical tag. You simply pay for your tag and the payment is recorded. When firefighters are called to a property, they will *not* look for a tag first. They will fight the fire regardless of whether or not the tag has been paid.

If you do not pay for your fire tag, some places, according to state laws, will charge you as much as $10,000 per hour, per man, to fight your fire. You can do the math. At $10,000 times a couple of hours and maybe 10 or 15 fire fighters, it can really add up.

Whether or not you experience a fire, failure to pay this fire tag will result in the district placing a lien on your property. These liens can be very substantial.

As a property investor, the existence of such a lien can be a very rude awakening. It can take all the profit right out of your deal. There usually is not too much to worry about with vacant lots. However, a fire lien can come into play if there was a structure previously located on the property.

Some other liens that I have run into over the years include *grass cutting* and *weed abatement* liens. These liens almost always come up at the time you are paying the back taxes.

When properties are left vacant and uncared for, the cities, counties or municipalities will sometimes cut the grass and take care of other nuisances that may arise. Some places will cut the grass simply to keep the place from looking bad in an otherwise well-kept neighborhood.

For larger properties, grass cutting charges can be as high as $300 per cutting—sometimes even more! Add this up over several years of someone not paying their taxes and you get the picture.

Grass cutting and weed abatement liens can ruin your deal. I have yet to see a municipality that will waive these liens so I've always had to pay them. I usually come out pretty well in the end, despite these added costs. I just want to know about them before I get too far into the purchase of a property.

Mechanics liens are another type of lien that may come up. If a contractor performed some work on the property and did not get paid, they may put a *mechanics lien* on the property. This makes sense; after all, they did the work and they are entitled to get paid for it.

A few years ago, I bought several pieces of property at once and found out that two of them had liens for *more than $10,000,000* on them! It turned out that these properties, as well as several others, were tied together with a large construction project that was since defunct.

The construction company, which was long out of business, had never released the liens. This is not uncommon these days. With all of the property foreclosures and companies merging, changing names or going out of business, this sort of situation comes up fairly often.

So, what did I do? I got the title cleared and sold the property. This was done with by means of a *Quiet Title law suit*. I'll describe how I do this later.

Besides all of the liens mentioned above (which are the most common) there are many other types that can, and will, show up from time to time.

Be aware, however, that even if no liens show up on the property, you may still have issues with obtaining a *clean title.* There may be *heirs* involved. This is the case with many of the properties that I have bought for back taxes. If the property had been owned by someone who has since passed away, it is possible that the heirs are unaware that the property is part of the decedent's estate. Years later, they might try to claim their property.

So why would I want to buy a property for back taxes that could have a title that is not free and clear? Naturally, I don't. The only way I know of to get a guaranteed clear title is through a *Quiet Title law suit* in a civil court. A Quiet Title law suit gives anyone that may have an interest in the property the opportunity to show up in court to present their case.

I am not an attorney and will not give you any legal advice. Each area is different and has its own filing procedures. You need to find out what the rules are where you live. I highly recommend that you seek the counsel of an attorney that specializes in real estate in your county. It is never a good idea to file a Quiet Title law suit on your own.

The procedure for filing a Quiet Title law suit generally goes something like this:

You will order and receive a *Title Letter Report* from a local title company. These usually do not cost too much. I typically pay between $125 and $200 to obtain them.

The Title Letter Report will show all the liens that are on the title. This includes things like mortgage liens, association liens, municipality liens, mechanic liens, heirs, etc. This is not a complete title search; though it does show you who is possibly involved with the property.

To ensure that you have a clear title, each of these liens needs to be addressed. Every county is a little different in their procedures and you will need to follow their rules.

Some things that are usually required include notifying all of the lien holders and heirs that you have an interest in the property. These notices are typically sent via registered mail for which the recipients must sign to acknowledge receipt.

In many cases, a notice must be published in a local paper for a certain period of time, such as six weeks. This usually gives anyone with an interest in the property enough time to submit a *claim* to that effect.

After following all of the rules and procedures, you will be given a court date for your case. On this date, everyone who has been notified will have the opportunity to appear in court to state their case about why you should not get a free and clear title.

I have never had an instance where an interested party has shown up. In fact, my attorney told me that in more than 40 years of practicing real estate law, he has never seen anyone show up in court to challenge a Quiet Title lawsuit!

You can save a lot of time and money if you combine several Quiet Title law suits into one hearing—if, that is, your attorney will do it and the court allows it.

I had one Quiet Title law suit in which I combined 13 properties. There were 53 possible defendants; in addition to the many heirs, this included several mortgage companies including Wells Fargo, Bank of America and some local banks. There were also municipalities and property associations involved.

The bailiff jokingly gave my attorney a hard time about it. She had to go into the hall and announce the individual names of everyone involved in the suit. Not a single one of the parties who had an interest in any of the properties showed up!

All of the mortgages were waived, association dues were waived, the mechanics liens were waived (including the $10,000,000 lien mentioned earlier) and the heirs' interests were waived. I walked out of court that day with thirteen free and clear property titles!

Chapter Nine

A Short Story In-deed-s

JUST AS TREASURES ARE UNCOVERED FROM THE EARTH, SO VIRTUE APPEARS FROM GOOD DEEDS, AND WISDOM APPEARS FROM A PURE AND PEACEFUL MIND. TO WALK SAFELY THROUGH THE MAZE OF HUMAN LIFE, ONE NEEDS THE LIGHT OF WISDOM AND THE GUIDANCE OF VIRTUE...~BUDDHA~...

There are several types of deeds that I deal with. The *deed* conveys (transfers) ownership of a property from one party to another. The parties are called the *Grantee* and the *Grantor*.

The Grantee is the party transferring the property, and the Grantor is the party receiving it. Both parties will be specified by name on the deed along with their addresses and their counties of residence.

The property's *legal description* will also be spelled out on the deed. This description will usually include the lot and plat numbers. It may or may not include a physical address, i.e. 101 Main Street. It will usually have a *locator number* listed as well. The locator number is an abbreviation of the original survey that laid out the land.

Besides the state and county information, the deed will also include the *township locator, a map sheet index, a ¼ section index* and an *insert.*

It can seem a little confusing at first—especially since every county uses its own system. Some use all numbers with dashes in between, and some use letters and numbers with or without dashes.

Then, as if to confuse matters even more, many county and community maps use different numbers from each other. Most plat maps that can be obtained from the county will include both sets of numbers. It doesn't take too much effort to figure out their systems.

The deed will usually specify some kind of consideration between the Grantor and Grantee. *Consideration* is the term used to designate what is given in exchange for the property. This may or may not be an actual dollar amount.

When purchasing properties *over the counter* from the county, you will usually find the exact sale price listed on the deed. When buying or selling a property from someone other than a government entity, it will usually be more generic.

It's very common for the consideration to read something like this:

> said Grantor(s), for and in consideration of Ten Dollars ($10) and other valuable considerations paid by the said Grantee(s), etc.

I have included some examples with the paperwork.

The deed will also show the date of transfer as well as the *book* and *page number* where the deed is recorded with the county. There is a lot of other legal wording included on these deeds, most of which is not important for our purposes.

Deeds You Are Apt to Encounter when Buying from a County

A *Trustee's Deed* is a very common type of deed that counties use to convey ownership of a property to you. It specifies the Grantor, Grantee, legal description of the property and consideration.

Some counties may transfer ownership using a *Collector's Deed for Taxes.* This type of deed has the same general information as a Trustee's Deed.

Still other counties use a variation of deed types. Some counties I have bought from use a *Trustee's Deed Under Collector's Third Tax Sale*, or a *Collector's Deed for Lands Sold for Delinquent Taxes after Third Sale.*

These are some of the more common deeds that I've run into, though there are several more. In each case, these deeds convey ownership of the property from the county to you. That is all that really matters, no matter what they choose to call them.

Deeds that Convey Properties from You to the New Owners

There are a number of basic deeds that can be used to convey ownership of properties from you to others. The three that are most commonly used and are easiest to understand include the Quit Claim Deed, the General Warranty Deed, and the Special Warranty Deed.

A **Quit Claim Deed** is the one that is used most frequently in private-party property transfers. It simply conveys whatever interest one party has in a certain property to another party. Be aware that this includes the good, the bad and the ugly; if there are any issues with the title, the recipient will inherit responsibility for them.

A **General Warranty Deed** is another very commonly used deed when transferring property. A GWD is usually used in association with a property that is being sold through bank financing. This is a fully-guaranteed deed. It states that the Grantor will warrant and defend title to the property all the way back to when the land was first surveyed. Many times *Title Insurance* will be bought to further guarantee that the property is *free* and *clear.*

A **Special Warranty Deed** is the type of deed frequently used when banks sell their *REO's* (Real Estate Owned) and foreclosed properties. This type of deed guarantees that the current property owner did not do anything to cloud the title during their ownership. It does *not* guarantee the property back to the time the land was first surveyed.

The Special Warranty Deed is my deed of choice. It is not as limited as a Quit Claim Deed and it includes some guarantees. It is both simple to understand and easy to have recorded.

I prepare almost all of my deeds on my own and send them to the recorder myself. I keep a copy on my computer so I can make any necessary changes very quickly and easily. The Special Warranty Deed that I use is only two pages long. This makes it cost less to record than longer deeds since most counties charge by the number of pages that are recorded.

Deeds need to be verified and notarized by a *Notary Public* before they can be recorded. This is a simple process that can usually be done, at no charge to you, at your local bank. Most banks have a Notary Public in-house for their customers' financial notary needs.

If, for some reason, your bank cannot act as your notary, there are other notaries around. They are likely to charge you a fee, though it usually is no more than a couple of dollars.

I frequently take several deeds to the notary at one time. This saves me time by cutting down on the number of trips I must make to the bank, and it saves the notary a bit of time as well.

Each county has its own recording rules. For example, there are usually a minimum number of inches that must be left blank on the top and bottom of the document. This is so that the county officials have room to put their recording stamps, dates, etc. on the deed.

Also, some counties may require you to include a cover page with your deed. This will be recorded along with the deed and will add to the cost, if you are charged per page.

It is important to know the rules and procedures of each county you deal with. You do not want to have deeds sent back to you for not following the rules and/or for making mistakes.

Speaking of *mistakes,* yes I have made a few over the years. What do you do what that happens? First of all, don't panic.

The first time I made a mistake on a deed, it kept me up all night. The next morning I called a friend of mine who worked for a title company. Sensing my panic, she laughed and told me not to worry about it. Mistakes do come up from time to time, and there is a document for dealing with such things.

An *Affidavit of Scrivener's Error* can be filed with the county to make any necessary corrections. On it, you state both the incorrect information that was included on the original deed and the corrections that need to be made to it. This will be recorded on the property in question.

I have used the Affidavit of Scrivener's Error on a few occasions, though I do not want to make a habit of it. By double checking the property information as well as the parties involved, most mistakes can be avoided. There is also an additional fee required to record the correction. I don't like extra fees.

I have included some examples of the deeds that I use throughout this book. You are welcome to use them. Make sure you check with the county where you will be filing them to ensure that the forms you use are *legal* for that county. By doing this paperwork yourself, you are saving a lot of valuable time and money.

Chapter Ten

A Powerful, Fast and Easy Marketing Plan to Start Now

ATTRACT.ENGAGE.CONVERT..~LEE ODDEN~...

Marketing and sales are the most important skills you can ever have. It does not matter what business you are in. You have to be able to sell your *widgets*.

I have learned to be a good negotiator. This is not really a real-estate business; it is a people business. What? Yes, that's right. Even if you do your business strictly via the internet, you are still dealing with people.

We really are all the same. I've learned to never underestimate people or think that they do not measure up. I always treat every person I encounter with the utmost respect.

Everyone has to *win* in the negotiations I put together; otherwise it is not a good deal and I will not do it. I want everyone I do business with to feel good about having dealt with me.

I am constantly working on becoming an *expert* in marketing and sales. I continuously watch what others are doing, and when I like their ideas, *I borrow them*.

Good marketing skills lead to good cash flow, which is the lifeline of the real estate business. And, as I stated in Chapter Seven, *Cash Flow is King!* By mastering marketing you will directly affect your cash flow.

One of the most important aspects I need to decide before buying a property is what I'm going to do with it. What is my *exit strategy?*

Anyone can buy a property for back taxes. So once you have it, what are you going to do with it? Are you going to sell it for cash? Are you going to fix it up and rent it? Are you going to keep it for yourself? You need to know ahead of time what the heck you are going to do with it.

The last thing I want is to have a bunch of properties sitting around collecting dust and costing me money.

The tax bill will come around again each year. Trust me, they will not forget you!

My main exit strategy is to sell the properties as-is. Whether I sell them outright for cash or I finance them, I want to find a new buyer as quickly as possible. My plan is always to have a new buyer who will be responsible for the taxes before the next tax bill is due.

Effective marketing strategies change constantly over time. My strategy today is completely different than it was just a couple of years ago.

My Previous Strategy: Fast Sales through Auction Sites

I used to sell the majority of my properties on auction sites like *eBay* and *Overstock*.

In the heyday of the real estate boom, I would sell anywhere from ten to fifteen properties a week. There was always a nice supply of properties to be obtained from the counties—and there still is.

The counties processed the deeds fairly quickly, and I would usually have them in my possession within a couple of weeks. It was great. I would buy thirty, forty, or even fifty properties at a time. I would then put them up for auction, and they almost all always sold within a month.

There were hardly any non-payers. In the rare event that someone did not pay, they would receive a *non-payer strike* from eBay or the other auction venues.

If a non-payer got two or more strikes within a month, sellers could *block* these non-payers from placing bids. There really were not too many non-payers. Most bidders had complete integrity and honored their bids.

Another key factor on the auction sites was *feedback*. You could rate your transactions for others to see. Most ratings were posted fairly and reflected the experiences of both the buyers and the sellers. You could also write a few words of how the transaction went and anything else that could help a future buyer or seller.

Life was *good*. Then...eBay changed.

The CEO left. New management came in and started changing some of the rules. As mentioned previously, one of the first things that changed was that the site no longer required property auctions to be binding. In other words, those bidding on the auctions did not have to honor their bids!

What good is putting something up for auction when the high bidder is not obligated to pay?

There were now *no consequences* for winning an auction and not paying. You may be thinking, "Why not just leave *negative feedback* against the welchers?" After all, that would be the *honest* and *fair* thing to do.

Well, as it turns out, eBay changed the rules in regards to feedback as well. The *buyers* could still leave positive, negative or neutral feedback for the sellers. However, under the new rules, the sellers could only leave *positive* feedback!

Are you kidding me?

This completely took the honesty factor out of the online auctions. What good is any type of feedback if you can't tell the *truth?*

These changes caused a great deal of havoc for those of us who relied on the auction site for our marketing strategies. All of a sudden, I was facing issues with non-payers constantly. About half of the high bidders on my auctions failed to honor their bids. Some weeks, *none* of my high-bidders came through.

There were many properties that I had to list for auction, over and over—usually as many as five or six times, and sometimes even more! This ended up costing me a lot of money. You see, with auction sites such as eBay, you are charged a *listing fee* as well as a *final value* (selling) *fee*.

When a high-bidder fails to pay, eBay *will* reimburse your final value fee; however, they *will not* reimburse your listing fee. These listing fees can be quite high depending on the bells and whistles and warm-fuzzies that you choose to include as selling features.

In addition, it takes a while to get your final-value fee refunded. This is because the auction sites hold on to your money until the *non-paying dispute* is resolved.

These days, I still use sites like eBay, though not nearly as often. Auction sites are no longer the focus of my marketing strategy. Despite my issues with eBay, I do still want to keep my presence there. After all, the site does have some great benefits.

For example, one of the very nice things about sites like eBay is the worldwide exposure they can afford you. I have buyers in 47 U.S. states and at least 14 countries around the world, including Australia, China, the U.K., Germany, Israel, Canada, United Arab

Emirates, Japan, Iraq, South Africa, Greece, Belize, and Colombia.

My Strategy Today: Free Classifieds, Word-of-Mouth and Social Networking

I do things a little different these days. I have discovered many low and no-cost techniques that have proven effective for moving my properties.

- *Craigslist and Other Free Listing Sites*

I tend to use the free sites more than anything else. The main reason is their ease of use and their wide circulation. It takes about the same amount of time to set up the ads as it does on paid auction sites, and more buyers seem to be using these free classified sites every year.

I currently like to list a lot of ads on *Craigslist.* It is a good no-cost site where people can list just about everything. I particularly like it because they do not charge for real estate ad listings like the auction sites do.

Though it does not provide worldwide exposure like eBay does, Craigslist gives my ads very a broad national exposure. I have had buyers from all over the U.S. and Canada who have found my properties on Craigslist.

The formatting of ads on Craigslist is a bit more limited as well. The graphics and a few other things are more restricted. This doesn't really bother me since I'm really not that technical anyway, and it has not seemed to hinder my sales in any way.

One thing that I like to do is to do is include a link to my website in my ads. That way, I can attract a potential buyer's attention with just a few words of interest, and then, if they want more information, they can visit my website. While there, they may also view the other properties that I have for sale.

I run a variety of ads. Sometimes I'll post ads that include multiple properties. Other times I'll just advertise one property per ad. Another strategy I sometimes use is to be very generic and have interested parties contact me to request a *list* of all the properties that I currently have available.

I like to mix and match ads and keep them running at all times. I want people to contact me and ask for more information. I also want them to *ask me* to sell them my properties.

Many times I give just enough information in an ad to get potential buyers' attention so that they will be compelled to contact me to find out more.

This is a great way to talk to people and find out what, specifically, they are looking for. If I don't have exactly what they want right now, I might come across it later on down the road.

I like to take notes when I'm on the phone. My notes turn into my *future buyers list.* When I come across something I think one of these people might want, I get in touch with them.

My most popular call-back list is those who are looking for the *real fixer uppers.* For some reason there are a lot of people that want a weekend project for a low monthly payment.

- *Word-of-Mouth Marketing*

A big portion of my business these days comes from word of mouth. I believe this is still the best form of advertising. It's pretty common for me to get phone calls, emails or texts from a *referral* who wants to buy a property.

Sometimes these referrals already know a bit about the properties I have for sale and the terms I am offering. They contact me to find out more about lot and price specifics.

I have buyers from all over the world who have come to me because of a referral from another buyer. I attribute a big part of this to the way I do business. I like to sell a good property at a fair price and with great terms.

- *Facebook and Other Social Media*

In recent years social media has expanded to every corner of the globe. There are many social media sites that are prevalent today. I will be expounding on Facebook as it seems to be the most popular.

Just about *everyone* you know is on *Facebook.* Even my diehard "refusing to accept the modern era" friends are at least aware of it.

On Facebook, you set up a profile and choose the friends you wish to be connected with. You can post pictures and things that you want to say.

Social media should be approached with a bit of caution, however. Many people use these sites to post things they do not like, or things they just want to complain about. These posts do not go away.

Remember, anything that you post in cyber space is here to stay.

You may have heard stories about people not getting hired or losing jobs because of things they have posted on social media. Many employers today use sites such as Facebook as part of their screening process.

There have been school teachers that have lost their jobs because of something they posted, and school children who have had legal complications because of *cyber-bullying*.

Tattoos and social media posts are very similar. They should be considered thoughtfully as you will live with them for the rest of your life! Post wisely.

The way I approach Facebook is to post things that are enlightening and potentially beneficial to my friends. I do not post anything that is in any way *negative*.

I also never post anything when I'm upset or emotional about something, just as I do not respond to emails or phone calls until I'm calm and collected. I only want to post things that I feel would make my mother happy or proud.

The use of Facebook can be a good way to get your message out to the world. However, it is important to

197

realize that you cannot use your *personal* page for *business* purposes. If you put offers on your personal page you may get booted as this goes against the site's terms of service agreement.

If you wish to use Facebook to promote your business venture, you can set up a *fan page* or a *business page* that is connected to, but separate from, your personal page.

With a fan page, followers need to *opt-in* in order to follow your page. All of your opt-in friends will receive a notice when you post something. With a business page, people can choose to "like" it and will then see posts that you make on that page in their newsfeed.

This is a great way to stay in touch with past and potential clients and show them what you are doing. You can also show them what you have to offer.

I chose to create a fan page. On this page, I post positive affirmations and quotes, much like I do on my personal page. Here, I also promote my business.

One of the nice things about social media today is the way it is connected to other media. I have my page set up so that whenever I place an ad on eBay, it automatically posts on my Facebook fan page as well.

With some of the other sites I must post this information manually.

It is very simple to post things manually. I just *copy and paste* a link to the web site onto my page. A lot of sites will even include a little thumbnail picture with the post.

If someone wants more information about what I am offering, all they have to do is to click on the picture or the link, and they will be taken to my site. Even though I may not understand all the technology behind it, I find this it all to be pretty cool.

- *Paid Ads on Social Media*

I have not yet put paid ads on sites like Facebook. Even though I have checked them out, I have found that simply posting my properties on the free listing sites is working quite well for the time-being.

One of the really neat features of the paid ads is that they market specifically to people who may have an interest in what you have to sell. Ads appear on people's social media "news feeds" based on what they have looked at previously and the sorts of things that they have "liked" on their page.

It's a very ingenious way to market. I think *Google* pioneered this technology. Now almost all the social media sites use this method to customize their advertising toward the right demographic.

Using paid advertising on social media is no longer a shot in the dark. In the *old* days (i.e. just a couple of years ago), you simply ran an advertisement. You might have put your ad in local paper or some other periodical and then you would hope that it would be seen by the right people.

Today, ads can be very specific and sent to a very well-targeted market. The odds of a good ad working in your favor are therefore increased exponentially. The key, of course, is having a good advertisement.

- *The Power of YouTube*

Another great way to get your message out to the world is by posting a video on *YouTube.* YouTube is a free site where anyone with an account can upload videos.

A lot of people post a lot of different kinds of videos on YouTube. It can be a great place to post videos that promote your business.

I like to connect my YouTube videos to my website and to my social media sites. This is very simple to do and enables me to promote my videos. A lot of credibility can be attained through having a good deal of exposure.

A word of caution regarding YouTube: It's a great place to promote your business. Just keep in mind that someone visiting your video can also view *all* of your other videos unless you set them up with privacy restrictions. You really don't want your customers to see a video you posted of your brother-in-law's bachelor party, for example.

What I'm saying here is to be aware of what you put on the internet. It can help you, hurt you, promote you or crush you. Remember: *A reputation can take a lifetime to establish and can be destroyed with one foolish act.*

Marketing and Sales: The Bottom Line

To be successful, the most important thing to do is become a master and an expert at *marketing* and *sales*. Marketing can make or break your business. The idea is to create enough cash flow for you to sustain your business and ensure success.

One of reasons that I focus on cash flow is because of the freedom it provides. When I reached the point where my monthly incoming cash flow exceeded my monthly expenses, my life changed for the better.

Because I have more money coming in than going out, I have time to do the things I really *want* to do. It does take a lot of work to get to this point; however, it is not *hard* work and it is not terribly time-consuming.

I have found it advantageous to work smart instead of working hard. I have also found that there is *no* get-rich-quick scheme that is right for me. The things I have come across that appear to be too good to be true are, in fact, exactly that.

There are many good books and trainings available to help you build your marketing skills. I like to take advantage of every one that I can. I have found that you can never learn too much. I know I must continually strive to be a great marketer.

By becoming a master at marketing you can master your world. And, really, who *doesn't* want to master their own world?

Chapter Eleven

Ultimate Beginners Guide to Succeed Today

YOU CAN LEARN NEW THINGS AT ANY TIME IN YOUR LIFE IF YOU'RE WILLING TO BE A BEGINNER. IF YOU ACTUALLY LEARN TO LIKE BEING A BEGINNER, THE WHOLE WORLD OPENS UP TO YOU...~BARBARA SHER~...

Winning Strategies for Deal'ionaires

One of the hardest things to do when embarking on something new is simply getting started. We can study all the data, read all the books and attend all of the trainings; however, unless we actually get off of the couch and do something, nothing will ever happen.

I do not want you to approach this as I did and end up with *analysis paralysis!* I want you to become a Deal'ionaire *now*! It took me way too much time to actually take the leap and get into the game.

Everything does not have to be perfect for you to get started. You will never have all of the answers. Rather, you will learn from every deal and every transaction. Look for the lesson and you will find it.

It does not have to take a long time for you to start creating your own *Deal'ionaire Empire*. When you start from scratch, you will be starting small, but you can keep things going until you have grown as big as you want. The first step, of course, is to simply get started.

We have a tremendous advantage today because of the internet. When I first started buying properties for back taxes, most of the counties did not have a website. Even today, there are still many counties that do not have especially good websites.

Surprisingly, I have found that some of the best websites that are out there today belong to some of the smaller and, maybe, less-likely counties. Some of these counties have spectacular websites that show everything from the history of the properties to aerial views from space that allow you to zoom in on a specific property.

How good the sites are depends on each individual county. Some are more *user friendly* than others and some include very useful research tools.

There are also some very informative websites available. One that I use more than any other is www.netronline.com. A few years ago, I paid quite a bit of money to go to a real estate seminar that was focused entirely on the many uses of this website. This money was well-spent as this site has proven very valuable to me.

Netronline.com has all kinds of real-estate information. Much of the information they offer is *pay-per-use* though there is also a lot of *free* information available to the public. I frequently access this free public information as it is extremely useful.

When you click on the *Public Records Online* link on netronline's home page, it will take you to a map of the United States. By selecting a state, you will be taken to a page that lists all the counties in that state.

If you then select a county, you will be taken to a page with that county's real estate-related contact information. This will usually include the Assessor's and Collector's phone numbers and web addresses (provided they have websites).

Some of the county websites will have all of the information you need to get started, though most will not. I usually have to make a phone call to get the information I need. It has been my experience that people who answer the phones at the courthouses are usually very nice.

As I mentioned earlier in the book, I sometimes have to make a few calls to the same county before I am able to find out if they have any of the types of properties I am looking for available for sale. If they do not have what I am looking for, I make a note to check back at a later date and move on.

When I am ready to approach the purchase of a new set of properties, the first thing I will do is to pick out an area and then *farm it*. I will usually look for a county that has lots of inventory, i.e. lots of properties available in a few areas. When farming the area, I am looking for properties that I can buy for a *good* price and then sell for a *great* price.

Once I choose where I want to farm, my next step is to learn all I can about the area. I want to find out if the properties are situated within city limits, or are part of a gated community with an association, or are in a rural location, etc. I'm also looking to see if there might be any extra charges and fees associated with owning the property, such as grass cutting and back association dues.

A good place to search after you have picked out a county is online using Google. I will usually Google the county, the area, the community and even the state where the property is located. There are usually some very good maps and images available.

Some communities have highly informative websites. Through them, I can find out a lot before I contact the city or Property Owners Association (POA) to find out about what fees may be owed on the particular properties I am interested in. I want to know about them *before* I buy so that I know what I am getting into.

For example, let's say I am looking at a property that I can buy for back taxes at a cost of $400 and that I can potentially sell for $3,500. If this property also comes with a grass cutting fee of $650 and a demolition fee of $10,000, this is something very important that I would want to know about.

While the grass cutting fee is manageable, the demolition fee would definitely be a deal killer. A demolition charge might come into play if a structure had previously existed on the property. For example, if a house were condemned due to neglect or fire damage and the owner failed to tear it down. In such a case, the community may have stepped in and done it themselves, charging a demolition fee in the process.

There are many reasons why homeowners just *walk away* from their properties. None of these reasons are good reasons in my opinion. It is an unfortunate thing that happens to some properties.

The owners may not have had homeowners insurance or may not have had adequate coverage to pay for the repairs or demolition. Or, it may have been a rental property that the owner just didn't care about any more.

There's absolutely nothing good that can become of a property that has a clouded title. Many times the property just sits there for years accumulating more taxes and more fees, such as grass cutting fees. It can take many years for the property to appreciate enough in value for someone to take on these exorbitant costs.

Fees and charges like this do come up and you need to be aware of them before you make a purchase. These charges are pretty easy to find out about. The county will usually be able to tell you, as will the city or municipality in which the property is located.

The most common fees I've seen are POA and HOA (homeowners association) fees. I have found that *most* (not all) POAs and HOAs can be persuaded to waive the back fees accumulated by the previous owner.

To facilitate this, I used to meet with a lot of POAs and HOAs and explained that they were currently receiving no dues on the property and that it would benefit them to waive the back fees so that a new owner can start paying future fees. I stressed the added benefit that new tax money will start coming in again as well.

Of course, there were, and are, always a few POAs, HOAs and communities that will not budge on these back fees. I don't know why, and in the end it is their loss. What good is a property that is just sitting there and not bringing in any money?

Today I no longer visit many POAs. Now, I simply call them on the phone. Most of the people in the offices are pretty easy to talk to and realize the value of *Deal'ionaires* like us who are bringing money to them. They are especially appreciative if they have several *non-paying* properties.

Steps to Take NOW

1) Choose the county and area that you would like to farm for properties.
2) Get on the internet and do some research.
3) Make the appropriate phone calls for doing your due diligence.
4) Buy a property and get in the game.
5) Start marketing your property.
6) Sell your property for cash or finance it.
7) Do it again!

You'll be glad you did!

Happy Investing!

From One

Deal'ionaire to Another!

Glossary

And Other Assorted Insomniac Reading

WHEN I CAN'T SLEEP, I TRY COUNTING SHEEP, BUT MY ADD KICKS IN, ONE SHEEP, TWO SHEEP, COW, PIG, OLD MACDONALD HAD A FARM, HEY MACARENA!...~SOMEECARDS~~

Abandon – to relinquish the rights of property ownership

Abstract of Title – a historical summary of all the recorded transactions that affect the title to the property

Addendum – clause that is added to the end of the contract and which supersedes what is written in the contract

Agent – someone who acts on behalf of another for a fee. In real estate, the term refers to a person with a real estate license who works under the authority of a real estate broker

Agreement of Sale – a written, signed agreement between the seller and purchaser in which the purchaser agrees to buy certain real estate and the seller agrees to transfer the property once the buyer meets the terms of the agreement; also referred to as a contract of purchase, a purchase agreement, and offer and acceptance, an earnest money contract or a sales agreement

Amortization – a gradual paying off of a debt via regular periodic installments which pay toward the principal and interest over a specified period of time

Annual Percentage Rate (APR) – the effective rate of interest for a loan per year

Appraisal – an opinion or estimate of the value of a property on a given date

Appreciation – increase in the value of a property

Arm's Length Transaction – a transaction between two related or affiliated parties that is conducted as though they were unrelated, so that there is no question of a conflict of interest

Arrears – the amount of debt that is overdue or unpaid; a payment that is made past its due date

Assessment – a local tax levied against a property for a specific purpose, i.e. street lights, sewer laterals, etc.

Assessor – a judge or magistrate's assistant who sets the tax values levied against the real estate

Asset – anything of value that can be converted into cash or used to pay a debt

Assign – to transfer interest

Assignee – individual to whom a title, claim, property, interest, or right has been transferred

Assignor – the party that transfers a title, claim, property, interest, or right to another party

Assignment Clause – a sales contract with an assignment clause allows the buyer to transfer the interest in the property (e.g. the right to buy it at the given rates and terms) to another party.

Bankruptcy – a state of insolvency; a position where a debtor who is unable to meet his/her financial obligations seeks debt relief through the courts; bankruptcy is typically accompanied by a surrendering of assets and affects an individual's credit report for at least seven years

Beneficiary – the person who receives, or is eligible to receive, the benefits resulting from certain acts

Bid – an offer of a specific amount of money in exchange for products and services, as in an auction

Borrower (Mortgagor) – one who applies, or has applied, for a loan secured by real estate and who is responsible for repaying the loan (mortgage)

Broker – an individual or firm that acts as ab intermediary between a buyer and seller while usually charging a commission

Capital – money used to generate income

Capital Gains – profit earned through the sale of real estate, or the amount by which an asset's selling price exceeds its initial purchase price

Capitalization Rate – the rate used to determine the present value of a property with future earnings potential

Cash Flow – cash derived over a certain period of time from an income-producing property; cash receipts minus cash payments over a certain period of time

Caveat Emptor – a legal term meaning "let the buyer beware;" indicates that the buyer must examine the property and buy at his or her own risk, i.e. a property may be offered in "as-is" condition with no expressed or implied guarantee of condition, quality, etc.

Certificate of Occupancy – document issued by a local governmental agency that states that a property meets the local building standards for occupancy and is in compliance with public health and building codes

Certificate of Title – an opinion rendered by an attorney as to the status of title to a property, according to the public records; this certificate does not hold the same level of protection as title insurance

Chain of Title – chronological order of conveyance of a parcel of land from the original owner to the present owner; an Abstractor can research the chain of title to a property going back to the date that the property was granted to the United States

Chattel – any personal, tangible, or movable property; non-real-estate personal property

Clear Title – a marketable title, free of liens and without legal questions as to the ownership of the property; most lenders require a clear title prior to closing

Closing – 1) the act of transferring ownership of a property from a seller to buyer in accordance with a sales contract; 2) the time when a closing takes place; 3) the process of signing the documents required to transfer ownership of a property

Closing Costs – expenses incurred by the buyer and seller in a real estate or mortgage transaction that are over and above the price of the property; these are made u of pro-rated cost including *non-recurring costs* (such as discount and origination points, lender's fees, title insurance fees, escrow, attorney or closing agent fees, recording fees, inspection and appraisal fees, and real estate brokerage commissions) and *recurring costs* (such as hazard insurance, interest, property taxes, mortgage insurance, and association fees)

Closing Statement – a settlement statement that discloses all of the financial information pertaining to the transaction for the buyer and seller, including all costs

Cloud on Title – an outstanding claim or encumbrance that, if valid, would affect or impair the owner's title

Collateral – assets that are pledged by a borrower to secure a loan or other credit and that are subject to seizure in the event of a default

Commission – the fee charged by a broker or agent when selling real estate

Comparative Marketing Analysis (CMA) – a comparison of sales prices of similar properties in a given area for the purpose of determining the fair market value of a property; also commonly referred to as "Comps"

Consideration – anything of value that is given to induce another to enter into a contract; includes an earnest money deposit on a sales contract

Contract – a binding agreement between competent parties; to have a valid contract for the sale of real estate, there must be 1) an offer, 2) an acceptance, 3) competent parties, 4) consideration, 5) legal purpose, 6) written documentation, 7) a description of property, and 8) signatures by principals or their attorney-in-fact

Contract for Deed - a contract between a seller and buyer of real property in which the seller provides financing to buy the property for an agreed-upon purchase price and the buyer repays the loan in installments; also referred to as a land contract, an agreement for deed, or an installment sale agreement

County – a political and administrative division of a state that provides certain local governmental services

County Seat – an administrative center, or seat of government, for a county or civil parish

Courthouse – a building that is home to a local court of law and often the regional county government as well

Covenant – a written agreement or restriction on the use of land, or promising certain acts; Homeowners Associations often enforce restrictive covenants governing architectural controls and maintenance responsibilities; however land can also be subject to restrictive covenants even if there is no homeowners association

Deed – a written document by which title to real property is transferred from one owner to another.

Deed Restriction – a clause in the deed that limits the use of the land; for example, a deed might require that a road may not be built on the property

218

Default – failure to meet legal obligations in a contract such as not making the agreed-upon monthly payments

Disclosure – statement of fact(s) concerning the condition of a property for that is up for sale as well as the surrounding area

Due Diligence – 1) an investigation or audit of a potential investment that serves to confirm all material facts in regards to a sale; 2) the care a reasonable person should take before entering into an agreement or a transaction with another party

Easement – the right to use the land of another for a specific purpose either for a temporary or a permanent amount of time; for example, a utility company may need an easement to run electric lines through a property

Eminent Domain – the right of the government or a public utility to acquire private property for public use by condemnation, with proper compensation given to the property owner

Encumbrance – a legal right or interest in land that affects a good or clear title, and diminishes the land's value; examples include zoning ordinances, easement rights, claims, mortgages, liens, charges, pending legal actions, unpaid taxes, and restrictive covenants

Free and Clear Property – a property that has no liens

General Warranty Deed – a deed that guarantees the title when transferring a property from a seller to a buyer

Grace Period – the time period between the date a payment is due and the date on which late charges will be assessed, for example, payments due on the 1st day of the month may have a 14 day grace period, meaning that fees will be charged if payment is not received by the 15th

Grantee – in a deed, the party who is designated as the buyer, or recipient

Grantor – in a deed, the party that is designated as the seller, or giver

Homeowners Association (HOA) – An association of homeowners that oversees the common areas of a development and enforces its rules and regulations; see also Property Owner Association (POA)

Income Property – real estate that generates income

Inspection – an examination of a property or building to determine its condition or quality either for a particular purpose or to confirm that the property meets the standards of the contract

Interest Rate – the percentage rate at which a principle amount will charged by a lender for the use of the funds

Investor – a money source for a lender; also, one who makes investments

Land Trust – a trust that is used to protect the assets of an individual and on which only trustee, not the beneficiary, is named in public records

Lien – a claim against a property for the purpose of collecting unpaid debts, judgments, mortgage payments or taxes

Market Value – the highest amount for which something can be sold in a given market

Mortgage – a written legal agreement that creates a lien against a property as security for the payment of a debt; a loan taken out to pay for real estate and that usually includes agreed upon interest rates and a payment schedule.

Mortgagee – the lender in a mortgage; typically a bank

Mortgagor – the borrower in a mortgage; typically a home or property owner

Multiple Listing Service (MLS) – a group of brokers that has joined together in a marketing organization for the purpose of pooling their respective listings; in exchange for a potentially larger audience of buyers, the brokers will agree to share commissions

Note – a legal document that obligates a borrower to repay a loan at a specified interest rate during a specified period of time, or on demand

Oral Contract – a verbal agreement that is typically unenforceable

Owner of Record – the individual named on a deed that has been recorded at the county recorder's office

Prepayment – full or partial payment to the principal of a loan that is made before the designated due date

Prepayment Penalty – an amount charged for an early payoff of a loan

Promissory Note – a signed legal document that acknowledges the existence of a debt and the borrowers promise to repay it

Property Owners Association (POA) – an association that oversees the common areas of a property development and enforces its rules and regulations; see also Homeowner's Association (HOA)

Public Sale – a property auction that is open to the general public; a public sale generally requires notice (advertising) and must be held in a place accessible to the general public

Purchase – to obtain property in exchange for money

Quiet Title (Action) – a court action that establishes ownership of property

Quit Claim Deed – a deed that transfers, with no warranties on the title, whatever interest the maker of the deed may have in a particular parcel of land to the possession of another party

Real Estate Broker – an individual who is licensed to arrange the buying and selling of real estate for a fee

Real Property – land, including trees, minerals and any permanent fixtures attached to it

Realtor – a real estate professional who is a member of the National Association of Realtors

Recording – the act of entering into a book of public records any instruments or documentation that affects the title to a real property

Recording Fees – money paid to the county recorder to record a deed, mortgage, trust, etc.

Restrictive Covenants – Private restrictions limiting the use of real property that are created by deed and may "run with the land," therefore binding all subsequent purchasers of the land; or that may be personal and binding only between the seller and buyer

Right of First Refusal – the right to purchase a property under the same terms and conditions that were made by another buyer and accepted by the seller

Seller Financing – an arrangement in which the seller of a property agrees to hold the mortgage and accept monthly payments instead of receiving payment in one lump sum

Special Warranty Deed – a deed in which the grantor does not warrant against title defects arising from conditions that existed before he/she took ownership of the property and in which the grantor warrants that he/she has done nothing to impair the title

Tax Lien – a lien imposed on a property for nonpayment of taxes

Tax Sale – public sale of a property at auction by a government authority as a result of nonpayment of taxes

Title – a legal document establishing evidence of ownership

Title Insurance – an insurance policy that protects the insured against loss arising from a property owner dispute

Title Report – a document indicating the current state of title for a property; the report includes information on the current ownership, outstanding deeds of trust or mortgages, liens, easements, covenants, restrictions, and any known defects

Title Search – an examination of the public records to determine the ownership and encumbrances affecting a property

Tract – a parcel of land generally held for the purpose of subdivision

Trustee – a person who is given legal responsibility, via a Deed of Trust, to hold property in the best interest of or "for the benefit of" another

Unencumbered Property – real estate with a free and clear title

Unimproved Property – land that has not been developed

Warranty Deed – a deed that guarantees the title in a transfer of property from a seller to a buyer

Zoning – designating certain areas, or zones, for specific use, i.e. residential, commercial, agriculture; zoning ordinances are normally enforced by the city or the county

In his new book, **Secrets of a Deal'ionaire**, *John Lee* teaches unique strategies for buying real estate with little or no money. **Secrets of a Deal'ionaire** is the 21st century's new book of Nothing Down. He teaches how to obtain free properties from owners and how to buy property for a couple hundred dollars and turn it to thousands of dollars in profit with only two hours of work. It is a book that every real estate investor and entrepreneur that is interested in generating multiple streams of income should read.

~AJ Rassamni~
 Inventor
Entrepreneur
Author of *Gain the Unfair Advantage*
CEO MoneyMakerAcademy.com

I had no idea what I would find when I opened the attachment for your book. As I read, I kept thinking, John you are giving away some great secrets. Then I thought, the man knows what he is talking about, he has lived it. He should share it.

There is wealth in your thoughts and suggestions but also in the realization that one can trust the advice. The reader cannot escape the conclusion the author knows his subject matter.

You are my most enterprising client by developing a business out of the taxation of real property. I thought the government was the only one to make money out of taxes!

I was impressed.

~William B. Beedie~
Attorney

John sets the path to success with one step at a time. The small deals that John can help you acquire can add up to a huge portfolio. John is definitely on the cutting edge of real estate investing.

~Cynthia Schmidt~

(mrslandlady)

John is a very active in our organization and believes in honest dialogue and on-going education. John has openly reviewed his money making techniques with our members. I can say with first- hand experience that John is the real deal.

~ Jim Heisserer~

President of the St. Louis Real Estate Investors Association.

I have known John Lee, "The Deal'ionaire" for many years and I have always been amazed at how simple he makes inexpensive real estate purchases into a wonderful stream of income. His method works so well that people actually give him properties. I said that Correct!! They give him properties! I would recommend "The Deal'ionaire OTC System" of generating wealth through tax delinquent properties property acquisition as a way to generously supplement your income or make it your sole source of income. He has been one of the most popular interviewee's on This Week in Real Estate with Terry Hall and I always look forward to his visits. He's the REAL DEAL!

~Terry Hall~
International Radio Host of *This Week in Real Estate*

JOHN LEE

Secrets of a Deal'ionaire

According to US statistics over 1,000,000 Americans filed for bankruptcy last year. Over 85% could have been prevented if they had just $300 more per month. Would you like to know how to turn $200 into $2,000 in less than 2 hours worth of total work?

The secrets and strategies John share are unique and priceless. He has simplified processes that can be very complicated.

The small deals that he has done over the last 25 years you have just learned in a very easy to understand format. One of the most important things John has learned is to get a mentor and jump start your way to success. There are two ways to do things, the easy way or the hard way. A mentor will get you there the easy way. The hard way is to spend twenty five years learning it yourself.

The information you need to get started in small deals that can make you a handsome profit is in this book. Lots of small deals can change your life.

John offers a work shop *The Deal'ionaire OTC System©* for those who would like to get some deeper information. He also is currently working with a very limited number of students that want a one on one session.

Lee has a different approach on his selection process on who he works with. He has a short questionnaire that determines whether you and he are the right match to work together. When you would like a questionnaire to learn about going to a new level simply send a request to theDealionaire@gmail.com or ams826@yahoo.com

You'll Be Glad You Did!

34797303R00142

Made in the USA
San Bernardino, CA
07 June 2016